the photographer's guide to New Mexico

Where to Find Perfect Sh[...] [...] to Take Them

Efraín M. Padró

THE COUNTRYMAN PRESS
WOODSTOCK, VERMONT

ISBN 978-0-88150-811-6

Cover and interior photos by the author
Book design and composition by S. E. Livingston
Maps by Paul Woodward, © The Countryman Press

Published by The Countryman Press,
P.O. Box 748, Woodstock, Vermont 05091

Distributed by W. W. Norton & Company, Inc.,
500 Fifth Avenue, New York, NY 10110

Manufactured in China

10 9 8 7 6 5 4 3 2 1

Title Page: Shiprock (see p. 15)
Opposite: Chimney Rock, Ghost Ranch (see pp. 29–30)

To my parents, Lillian and Rubén

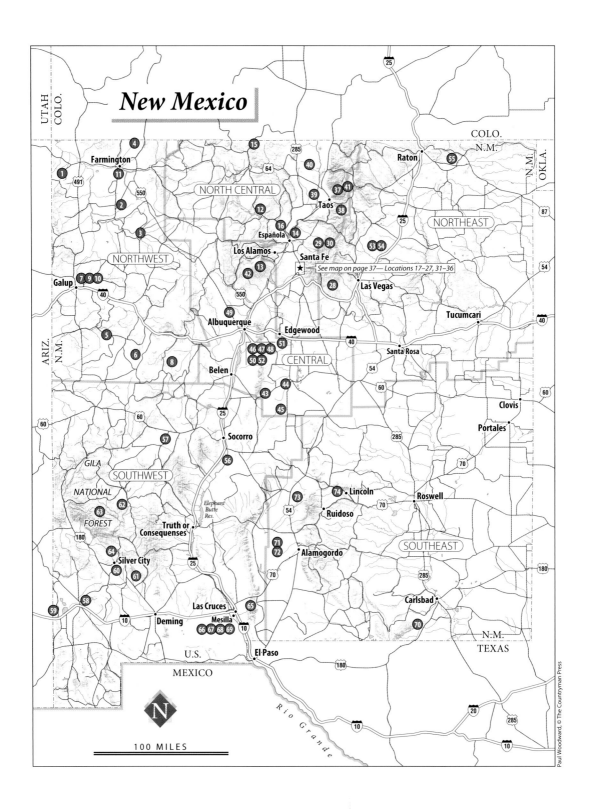

New Mexico

UTAH
COLO.

COLO.
N.M.

N.M.
OKLA.

① Farmington ⑪ ④ ⑮ ⑤⑤ Raton

②
③ NORTH CENTRAL ⑤⑤

NORTHWEST
Galup ⑦⑨⑩
⑫
⑯ ⑭ Española
⑲ ㉗ ⑪
Taos ㉘
⑯ NORTHEAST

Los Alamos ⑬
㉙㉚
Santa Fe ★
⑤③⑤④ Las Vegas

Tucumcari

⑭②
See map on page 37— Locations 17–27, 31–36
㉘

⑲
Albuquerque
Edgewood
⑤①
CENTRAL
Santa Rosa

⑤ ⑥ ⑧
Belen
⑭⑥⑭⑦⑭⑧
⑤⓪⑤②

Clovis
Portales

⑥⓪
⑥
Socorro
⑤⑦
⑤⑥
Elephant Butte Res.
㊸
㊹
㊺

GILA
NATIONAL
SOUTHWEST
⑥②
⑥③
FOREST
⑦③
⑦④ Lincoln
Roswell
㊴
Ruidoso

Truth or
Consequenses
⑥④
⑦①
⑦②
Alamogordo
SOUTHEAST

Silver City
⑥⓪
⑥①
Carlsbad
⑤⑧
⑤⑨
Las Cruces ⑥⑤
Deming Mesilla
⑥⑥⑥⑦⑥⑧⑥⑨
⑦⓪

N.M.
TEXAS

U.S.
MEXICO

El Paso

Rio Grande

N

100 MILES

Paul Woodward, © The Countryman Press

Contents

IV. Northeast New Mexico

Chile ristra, Old Mesilla

V. Southwest New Mexico

VI. Southeast New Mexico

Mexican dancers, 16 de Septiembre/Mexican Independence Day Celebration, Old Mesilla

Introduction

New Mexico is a land of photographic variety, mostly thanks to the state's location at the junction of four geologic provinces: the southern Rocky Mountains, the Great Plains, the Basin and Range Province, and the Colorado Plateau. Down the middle of it all lies a north-south sunken zone called the Rio Grande Rift. Within the state's borders landscape photographers will find snow-covered mountains and alpine lakes, deep canyons, colorful sandstone formations, cathedral-sized caverns, sensuous sand dunes, extinct volcanoes and lava flows, and badlands that defy description.

New Mexico is also home to some of the most impressive pre-Columbian rock art and architecture in the Southwest, offering the photographer many opportunities to explore and photograph ancient pueblos, kivas (under-ground ceremonial chambers), dwellings, and petroglyphs.

Other subjects of cultural importance include Spanish colonial architecture such as plazas, missions, and historic buildings; modern pueblos, some of which are open to the public; and the dazzling variety of fiestas, dances, and celebrations that take place in New Mexico all year long.

New Mexico also offers great photographic opportunities for bird photographers, train lovers, and those looking for E.T.

Regardless of what you like to photograph, the one constant in your New Mexico photo journeys will be the state's renowned beautiful, clear light, which has for centuries attracted artists such as Ansel Adams and Georgia O'Keeffe to the Land of Enchantment.

North House and Sangre de Cristo Mountains, Taos Pueblo

Using This Book

This is the first photography guide written exclusively about New Mexico, and in addition to photo-worthy locations it includes my favorite events to photograph, such as Albuquerque's International Balloon Fiesta and Old Mesilla's Cinco de Mayo Celebration. Because there is so much to photograph in the state, I have included only those locations and events I believe will yield the best photo ops after a reasonable amount of effort—no monster hikes here.

At the beginning of each chapter, I have included a general description of the region, logistical information, and a 4-star rating system (4 being the best) to help you determine the best times of the year to visit a particular area. Each chapter also includes a "Diversions" section with suggestions on what to do just for fun.

For ideas and recommendations on planning your photo trip, I have included a "Favorites" section at the end. Selecting my favorites was a highly subjective exercise, and my selections are intended to serve as guidelines to help you find your own special places.

Regardless of which regions of New Mexico you visit, I encourage you to have fun, explore past the obvious, and see what's around the next bend. As photojournalist Elliot Erwitt said, "It's about time we started to take photography seriously and treat it as a hobby."

How I Photograph New Mexico

Creativity is a messy, difficult, and time-consuming process. There is a big difference between the *idea* of taking a good photograph (romanticized by magazines such as *National Geographic*) and the reality of getting up at an uncivilized hour and driving in darkness to be at a bitter cold location at just the right time, with absolutely no guarantee of success.

There are many things you can do, however, to improve your chances of success in the field. These include research and preparation (more fun than it sounds), knowing about light and the weather, and equipment selection. And since this book includes a number of Indian dances and pueblos, I have also included a section about etiquette when photographing these subjects to help you get the most out of your visit.

Research and Preparation

Before I head out in the field I arm myself with information that will help me increase my chances of making good images. This entails reading books (such as this one), looking at tourism and Chamber of Commerce websites, and consulting with maps so I can visit different places in a more or less organized manner. I personally love learning about history, culture, and geology before I visit places, but I realize not everyone has the same inclination, so do as much research as you enjoy.

As I prepare myself for the trip I begin compiling a shooting list that will help me concentrate on the subjects I want to photograph. The shooting list is designed to serve only as a general guide, however, not a rigid mandate. The key is to stay flexible and open to other photo possibilities.

When I'm compiling my shooting list I also begin thinking about "photo themes," so that when I come home I have a cohesive set of images that would make a nice collection of prints, or a set of cards, and so on. In New Mexico you might want to feature, for example, images of missions, or perhaps pictures of desert landscapes. As with the shooting list, the themes list should serve only as a general guideline and should not be set in stone.

Light

The type of light falling on your subject will be one of the most important factors in determining whether your images are successful. In general, flat, dull light will produce flat, dull pictures. It is therefore important to recognize good light and be at the right place when the light is at its best.

New Mexico's light has a crisp, clean feel that is otherwise very difficult to describe. However, as with everywhere else, the warmest, most flattering light occurs early and late in the day. I prefer this early/late light for photographing landscapes and architecture, especially in places where there are no mountains to block the sun along the horizon. If there are clouds in the sky I also like to photograph while the sun is below the horizon, when the clouds' underside is bathed in pinks, reds, oranges, and purples. This soft light is also reflected on the landscape, and even though the eye has a hard time seeing the soft hues, your camera will capture them.

One of my favorite times to photograph architecture such as churches and cityscapes is at twilight, especially if the buildings are lit with floodlights. Typically, about 30–40 minutes after sundown (or before sunrise), the skies turn a rich cobalt blue that is well balanced with the light from the floodlights illuminating your subject. This window of opportunity usually lasts only about 15 minutes, so make sure you scout the location in advance. I check three things while evaluating these types of locations: where the lights are located (most buildings are illuminated from the front, but not all), whether the lights are working (so you don't waste a trip), and what times the lights are on (sometimes they are turned off around midnight, eliminating an early morning shoot as a possibility).

Many of the events described in this book take place during the harsh light of day, well after or before the light is most flattering. I usually hope for overcast conditions when photographing these events, as the clouds above act as a huge diffuser and reduce contrast. However, New Mexico has over 300 days of sunshine a year, so most of the time you will be photographing in high-contrast situations. In these cases I use fill flash to soften the shadows and reduce contrast caused by the unfiltered sunlight.

In addition to cooler temperatures, fall brings an exception to my early/late preference for photographing landscapes. During this season I usually extend my shooting sessions into midmorning (or begin in mid-afternoon) to capture the yellow aspen leaves at their most brilliant, as the sunlight shines right through the leaves.

Weather

New Mexico's weather can turn from sunny to stormy in a hurry, so it's important to check the weather report before going out. Although the storms brought by the summer monsoon season will often yield towering cloud formations that can sometimes dwarf even the landscape,

Church at Gran Quivira in snow, Salinas Pueblo Missions National Monument

providing a spectacular photo subject, be careful with approaching storms and stay out of their way. Typically the best times to photograph storms are when they are brewing and as they clear. Not only will photographing during these times be safer, but also breaking-up clouds often will be accompanied by dramatic shafts of light.

Suggested Equipment

My basic kit when photographing New Mexico includes one camera body (with a backup), a dedicated flash, and three zoom lenses: a 16–35mm wide angle, a 24–105mm "normal," and a 100–200mm telephoto. I use the first two lenses for most of my landscape and architectural photography, and the telephoto for events or to tightly frame an interesting section of a landscape. I put my equipment in a photo backpack most of the time, but when I'm photographing events I prefer a shoulder bag for easy access.

I use a tripod when photographing landscapes, architecture, or anything that does not move, like a photogenic abandoned truck or an interesting mural. I know tripods are cumbersome to use and can be heavy, but I always give making images my best effort. It makes no sense to get up early and spend time and money to get to a location, and then be lazy with technique.

I do not use a tripod, however, when I'm shooting dances or other fast-moving events. Instead, I use lenses with anti-shake technology and high shutter speeds/small aperture combinations. If the light is low, I also ratchet up my ISO to 400 or even 800, though I prefer to use the lowest ISO possible so my images have less noise (or "grain," to use a film term).

My filter bag is a small but important part of my photographic arsenal. I commonly use a polarizing filter when photographing landscapes and architecture. "Polarizers" reduce haze, help eliminate reflections, and increase the saturation in the sky. They are easy to use because by rotating the filter while looking through your viewfinder, you can see its effect in real time. However, go easy when using polarizers at altitude since they can make the skies look almost black. I also use my polarizer when photographing moving water, since using the filter (which is dark) cuts about two stops of light, a convenient way to achieve an attractive, silky look to the water.

The other type of filter I carry is the split neutral density filter. This square filter is "split" between a dark half (of neutral gray) and a clear half. I use it mostly for landscapes when I want to reduce the contrast between bright skies (covered by the dark half of the filter) and the usually darker foreground (covered by the clear half so it is not affected). Split neutral

Adobe bell tower, with polarizer

Adobe bell tower, without polarizer

density filters come in different strengths depending on how much light you need to block to get a balanced exposure. I carry one-, two-, and three-stop filters with me, and use the two-stop filter the most. The selected filter can be used by placing it in a holder which attaches to the lens, or (my preferred mode) by simply holding it in place while looking through your viewfinder.

Other items I carry while photographing in New Mexico include a GPS receiver and compass (to get my bearings while scouting or getting back to the car), a hot-shoe-mounted bubble level (to make sure my landscapes are straight), a cable release, a small flashlight, and a notepad and pen for writing subject information. If there is an interpretive sign near the subject I am photographing, I take a picture of the sign and use it for captioning my images later.

Etiquette When Photographing in Tribal Lands

Some of the places and events listed in this book are within Indian pueblos and reservations. And since photography is a very sensitive subject for Indians, here are some pointers to make your visit to tribal lands more productive and enjoyable.

Each pueblo and Indian reservation is a sovereign nation with its own government, laws, and visitor regulations. Know the rules—which are typically posted or available at a visitor center—and follow them. Expect to pay a camera fee in addition to an entry fee. Tripods are usually not allowed.

Remember that pueblos are villages with private homes. Do not wander inside any structure without permission unless it is obviously open to the public (like a church, although photography is usually forbidden inside them). Always ask before photographing a person or their crafts.

Acoma Pottery clay pots, Indian Market, Santa Fe. Always ask before taking pictures of Native Americans or their crafts.

Indian male dancer, pow wow, Gallup Inter-Tribal Ceremonial

I. Northwest New Mexico

SEASONAL RATINGS: SPRING ✦ ✦ ✦ ✦ SUMMER ✦ ✦ ✦ FALL ✦ ✦ ✦ ✦ WINTER ✦ ✦

General Description: Northwest New Mexico is Indian Country. A big portion of the largest Indian reservation in the United States, the Navajo Nation, is located here, together with the Jicarilla Apache Nation and the pueblos of Zuni, Acoma, and Laguna.

Despite the harsh desert conditions, hundreds of years ago the legendary Ancestral Pueblo civilizations (also known as the Anasazi) flourished in these parts, leaving behind an amazing array of dwellings and public buildings such as those found in Chaco Culture National Historical Park and Aztec Ruins National Monument. The region also offers the shutterbug a stark yet beautiful landscape of windswept badlands and deserts, plus a number of colorful events that are both fun to photograph and suited to the whole family.

Shiprock (1)

Located in New Mexico's extreme northwestern corner, Shiprock is a volcanic neck towering about 1,700 feet above the surrounding desert. According to legend, the Navajo came to these parts carried by the massive rock while fleeing from their enemies, thus giving the pinnacle its Navajo name, Tse Bi dahi, or "rock with wings." Shiprock is easily one of the most photographed natural formations in the state, and for good reason. Large and alone, massive and delicate, the peak and its sharp angles catch the beautiful New Mexico light in different ways depending on the time of day and year.

My favorite time to visit Shiprock is spring. Not only does the season bring milder temperatures, but also you will probably find colorful wildflowers to include in the foreground of your compositions. Fall is also pleasant, and I typically use surrounding volcanic rocks to

---

Noted For: Indian culture and ruins, badlands, volcanic formations, and expansive desert views

Best Times: Spring, fall, and during listed events

Exertion: Minimal to moderate

Peak Times: Spring: May; summer: June; fall: October; winter: December; during listed events

Facilities: At developed sites

Parking: In lots, on the street, and at trailheads

Sleeps and Eats: Farmington, Aztec, Bloomfield, Grants, Gallup, some in Cuba

Sites and Events Included: Shiprock, Bisti Wilderness Area, Chaco Culture National Historical Park, Aztec Ruins National Monument, El Morro National Monument, El Malpais National Monument, Red Rock State Park, Acoma Sky City, Gallup Inter-Tribal Indian Ceremonial, Red Rock Balloon Rally, Totah Festival Indian Market and Pow Wow

---

balance my pictures and "tell a story." A volcanic dike immediately south of the pinnacle is another option for a strong foreground subject, but be cautious if you climb the dike; there is no maintained trail and there are lots of jagged rocks.

Because Shiprock is exposed in every direction, it photographs well in either the morning or afternoon. I prefer the mornings because the parking area is on the east side of the dike, which nicely catches the day's first rays. In the afternoon I suggest driving around the pinnacle (first north on the dirt road, then west after you clear the rock) until you find a composition you like, then shoot from there.

You will need a wide-angle zoom (16–35mm, for example) to photograph Shiprock

Volcanic ridge and Shiprock

and its surroundings, and a medium telephoto zoom (up to 200mm or so) if you wish to fill the frame with the pinnacle only.

Directions: From the town of Shiprock, drive about 6.5 miles south on US 491 (formerly US 666), then turn right on NR 13 and travel another 8 miles. Just before a large wall of rock (the volcanic dike) meets the highway, turn right onto a rough dirt road. I usually drive on this road (going north) for about a mile or two before parking, then explore the area on foot. You can drive farther if you wish, but keep in mind the road is very rough in spots.

Bisti Wilderness Area (2)

Formed over millions of years by the slow accumulation of 14,000 feet of sedimentary rock, Bisti (pronounced "BIS-tie") is a collection of deeply eroded land forms including hoodoos (tall columns of oddly shaped rocks), spires, buttes, mushrooms, balancing rocks, washes, canyons, and natural sculptures that defy description. The 3,946-acre area is located less than 40 miles south of Farmington. Geologically speaking, however, this wilderness is as remote an area as a photographer is likely to explore. In 1996 Congress approved combining the Bisti Badlands with the much larger De-Na-Zin Wilderness Area to the east, but this section covers only Bisti, since in my opinion it is easier to reach and offers the best photo opportunities in the area.

There are no trails or designated overlooks in Bisti. Simply walk into the rocky wilderness and explore what looks interesting. I recommend using a compass or GPS to navigate the jumbled fantasyland that is Bisti; you should also wear a hat and carry plenty of water, as there are no services nearby.

To get you started, from the hiker's gate walk east for about 10–15 minutes along a wide wash surrounded by low eroded hills. After clearing a boundary fence to your left, begin hiking left (going north) until you reach a series of large mounds. Go up the mounds and take in the view. From here you should be able to see some interesting rock formations worth exploring and photographing. This hike will be an easy 2- to 3-mile round trip.

A more straightforward option is to walk east on the main wash for about 2 miles until you reach a large collection of rock formations. This hike is a little longer than the first one, but staying on the main wash makes it easier to retrace your steps to your car.

Because the landforms you will encounter are facing in all directions, either early morning or late afternoon will produce nicely lit subjects. Bring a wide-angle lens for grand landscape shots and to further distort the curved lines of some of the rocks you photograph. A midrange zoom will also come in handy to isolate details in the landscape. A polarizing filter will add definition to the clouds and intensity to the blue skies.

Directions: From Farmington head south on NM 371 for about 36 miles. After mile post 71 turn left onto CR 7297. Here the road turns into a graded dirt track passable by most vehicles. Follow the track for about 2 miles (staying left at a fork) to the Bisti parking area on your right. The area's entrance is marked with a sign, fence, hiker's gate, and sign-in box.

Rock on pedestal and badlands, Bisti Wilderness Area

Chaco Culture National Historical Park (3)

A UNESCO World Heritage Site since 1987, Chaco Culture National Historical Park (commonly referred to as Chaco Canyon) is located in a relatively remote wash near the center of the San Juan Basin region, about 60 miles from the nearest town. Chaco Canyon was an important Ancestral Puebloan cultural center from about A.D. 900 to 1130, and about 4,000 archaeological sites have been recorded within the park. Today, the biggest attractions to photographers are the "Chacoan great houses" (multistory stone buildings) and the many examples of prehistoric rock art scattered about the park, especially the well-known "supernova" pictograph.

All of Chaco's great houses can be reached from a well-paved 9-mile loop beginning and ending at the visitor center. My favorite houses are Pueblo Bonito (which can be photographed from above by climbing up a mesa), Chetro Ketl, and Casa Rinconada. Kin Kletso and Pueblo del Arroyo are also popular and photogenic. All of the great houses have small parking areas with toilets and can be reached via short, easy hikes of less than 0.5 mile.

Photo subjects include round ceremonial chambers known as "kivas," angular brick walls, rock art, doors leading to other doors, and ruined buildings photographed against the surrounding sandstone walls.

To reach the supernova pictograph involves a bigger effort. Follow the Peñasco Blanco Trail from the Pueblo del Arroyo parking lot for about 3.5 miles, passing Kin Kletso and a series of petroglyphs along the way. The trail is sandy, mostly level, and easy to follow, and as a bonus you'll get away from the most highly visited ar-

Aerial view, Pueblo Bonito in snow, Chaco Culture National Historical Park

eas. When you get to the supernova sign, look straight up to see it. Bring a mid-telephoto lens to take a frame-filling picture of the pictograph.

Because the park opens a few minutes before sunrise, it's important to scout a location beforehand so you know exactly where to be at first light. I typically photograph the outside of structures first, then move inside when the light becomes harsher. And since you will be able to get very close to the ruins (with a few roped-off exceptions), bring your wide-angle and normal-to-mid telephoto lenses. The afternoons offer excellent photo opportunities as well, though I prefer the mornings, as you will have the park to yourself for at least a couple of hours.

All trails close at sunset, but park rangers will give you a little extra time if you are in the middle of a shot.

Directions: From Bloomfield, drive south on US 550 about 47 miles to CR 7900. Turn right (west) and follow the signs another 21 miles to the entrance to Chaco Canyon. The last 13 miles are on a graded dirt road that is suitable for passenger cars (except when wet).

Aztec Ruins National Monument (4)

Despite its name, Aztec Ruins was built by the Ancestral Puebloan people around A.D. 1100 (19th-century archaeologists mistakenly believed that the ruins were built by the Aztecs from Mexico, thus the misnomer). Located in the modern city of Aztec, the park features a monumental great house that once held about 500 rooms, but the star of the show is a beautifully reconstructed "great kiva" over 40 feet in diameter, the only such structure in the Southwest. A short, paved walkway allows easy access to the ruins.

As you walk into the ruins after passing through the visitor center, go up the stairs in front of you for a panoramic view of the ruins

Interior of the great kiva (reconstructed), Aztec Ruins National Monument

from an overlook. Make note of the light quality and direction to help you visualize what kind of shots you will be taking. In general I use my wide-angle and mid-telephoto zooms in Aztec Ruins, since you will be able to get very close to your subjects.

After taking in the view, you follow the trail clockwise through the ruins, culminating in the reconstructed great kiva. If the light is harsh or conditions are otherwise not conducive to good photography, I simply make a bee line to the great kiva and spend most of my time photographing its interior. Otherwise I follow the trail, looking for interesting compositions of the brickwork, repeating door patterns, and other structures. Late fall is my favorite time to photograph Aztec Ruins, since the surrounding cottonwoods will add a colorful orange or yellow backdrop to your compositions.

The great kiva's interior has been carefully restored to its original condition, at least as interpreted by modern archaeologists. The partially sunken structure, with its simple architecture of large supporting beams, tall ceilings, and ceremonial basins, feels like a sanctuary

Yellow wildflowers and Inscription Rock, El Morro National Monument

similar to a church. Indeed, most archaeologists believe that kivas served a spiritual purpose.

Walk around the kiva for a few minutes before taking your first shot. This will slow you down and allow you to get a better feel for the subject. The chamber's many windows let in shafts of light, making for dramatic compositions that convey the sacred nature of the place. You will need a wide-angle lens to capture the kiva's large interior.

Directions: Aztec Ruins is located on Ruins Road, about 0.5 mile from NM 516 in the town of Aztec.

El Morro National Monument (5)

"Passed by here the Governor Don Juan de Oñate, from the discovery of the Sea of the South on the 16th of April, 1605." (Oñate was New Mexico's first governor, and the "Sea of the South" is the Gulf of California.) Thus reads (in Spanish) the oldest and most famous European inscription on Inscription Rock, El Morro National Monument's namesake formation ("morro" is Spanish for knoll or bulwark). For history buffs, that's 15 years before the Pilgrims first landed at Plymouth Rock. But Europeans were not the first people here by far. On Inscription Rock you will also find ancient petroglyphs, and on top of the park's mesa there is an Indian village the size of a city block, complete with living quarters and ceremonial kivas.

El Morro is a small park, making it easy to photograph its main attractions in a couple of hours. Although the park is closed during peak photography hours (early and late), Inscription Rock, a very photogenic rock formation that rises sharply from the surrounding plain, is visible from the roads surrounding the monument. One option is to photograph the rock from NM 53, which runs east and west on the monument's north side. From this location you can photograph Inscription Rock either early or late, using some of the surrounding trees and desert vegetation as foreground. The second option is to photograph the rock from the monument's access road, which travels in a north and south direction along its east flank. This makes for a very nice morning shot, as the sun turns the sandstone a brilliant salmon color. My favorite time to photograph this side is late summer, when a profusion of yellow wildflowers beautifully complements the red stone above. Use a split neutral density filter to reduce contrast when the sun hits the rock but before it reaches the flowers.

Inside the park, 2-mile-long Mesa Top Trail takes you through all the photo highlights El Morro has to offer. The trail is mostly paved and easy, but it does have a steep section leading to the mesa top 200 feet above. Traveling in a counter-clockwise direction, first head towards Inscription Loop Trail, which affords up-close-and-personal views of Inscription Rock before leading you to the many inscriptions left by passersby from long ago. A cloudy day will be ideal to photograph the inscriptions, as diffused light will reduce the sun's glare on the sandstone. You can also bring a large diffuser to block the sun as you photograph the inscriptions. A polarizer filter will also help with reducing reflections.

From atop the mesa the views of the surrounding valley are spectacular. Here you can photograph Inscription Rock from above, as well get a bird's-eye view of Box Canyon, a small but pretty canyon right in the middle of the park. Before you start your descent to the visitor center you will come across the ruins of A'ts'ina, a pre-Columbian village that was occupied during the 13th and 14th centuries. Here you can capture intimate views of the site's different rooms and kivas, as well as panoramic compositions using the ruins as foreground balanced by the grand landscapes surrounding the mesa.

Directions: From Grants, take NM 53 (Exit 81 off I-40) south for 41 miles to El Morro. From Gallup, take NM 602 (Exit 20 off I-40) south for about 31 miles. Turn east (left) on NM 53 and drive an additional 25 miles to the park.

El Malpais National Monument/National Conservation Area (6)

El Malpais ("badlands" in Spanish) features a vast lava field, complete with lava tubes and lava types with Hawaiian names like pahoehoe (smooth and rope-like) and a'a (sharp and jagged). Many landscape features in El Malpais bear these terms because early scientific knowledge of volcanoes developed in the Hawaiian Islands.

Along the east side of the monument, 500-foot sandstone cliffs mark the end of the lava flow and offer great opportunities to photograph these two geologic features together. A series of trails allow access to both the lava field and sandstone cliffs.

The single most photogenic spot in El Malpais is the Sandstone Bluffs Overlook. The overlook is located on the east side of the monument off NM 117, about 16 miles from Grants. The last 1.5 miles or so are on a graded dirt road suitable for cars.

The overlook offers tremendous views of the surrounding landscape, including expansive vistas of the lava flow to the west; Mount Taylor (11,301 feet), an eroded volcano, to the north; and impressive sandstone cliffs at your feet. Because the lava flows, though impressive, are difficult to photograph to good effect (they are black), this is a good spot to include them in a composition that features the sandstone bluff. The sandstone wall faces roughly west, so the best time to photograph it is late afternoon, when the sun's last rays make the sandstone bluff look like it's aglow in orange from within. Mornings also offer good opportunities to photograph the many sandstone formations

Sandstone Bluffs Overlook, El Malpais

atop the bluff, either against the (hopefully) beautiful sky, or again with the lava flows in the background.

About 8 miles south of the turnoff for the Sandstone Bluffs Overlook is La Ventana Natural Arch; at 125 feet high and 165 feet across at the base, it is one of the largest arches in New Mexico. Because of its orientation, the arch is best photographed in late afternoon. Make sure to get close enough to photograph La Ventana from below, as this will allow you to include some sky in the composition and show the arch in all its massive beauty.

Directions: Take I-40's Exit 89, just east of Grants, and drive south on NM 117, which marks the monument's eastern boundary. Both the Sandstone Bluffs Overlook and La Ventana Arch are accessed from NM 117.

Red Rock State Park (7)
Despite its name, Red Rock State Park is operated by the city of Gallup and is no longer part of the New Mexico State Parks system. This 640-acre park is home to massive red rock amphitheaters that began forming over 200 million years ago during the time of the dinosaurs. The park's main attractions are the distinctive sandstone formations and canyons that cut through the area. Red Rock is also the venue for a number of special events. Two of those events—the Gallup Inter-Tribal Indian Ceremonial and the Red Rock Balloon Rally—are featured later in this chapter.

The best way to photograph Red Rock's natural wonders is to hike the short (about 3 miles round trip) Pyramid Rock Trail leading to Pyramid Rock. This easy-to-follow but sometimes steep trail ascends almost 900 feet to the top of Pyramid Rock. From here the surrounding views are spectacular, though much of the panorama is cluttered with train tracks, factories, houses, and roads. I therefore suggest

Pyramid Rock, Red Rock State Park

focusing your attention on the distinctive shapes of Pyramid Rock (7,487 feet), which photographs best from the trail in the morning, and the sandstone spires of Church Rock, which look great in the afternoon. When photographing these and other rock formations in the park, use a tripod for tack-sharp images and a polarizer filter to increase the sky's saturation.

White ladders and ceremonial kivas, Sky City, Acoma Pueblo

To capture images of Pyramid Rock, hike about halfway up the trail and begin looking for interesting foreground subjects (rocks, trees, canyons) to include in your compositions. I recommend using a wide-angle lens for these shots. To reach the trailhead for Pyramid Trail, follow the signs once you enter the park.

Although Church Rock can also be seen from Pyramid Trail, you can get closer to it and achieve different angles by following the easy, 2-mile Church Rock Trail, which roughly follows a red rock canyon floor. The trailhead for Church Rock Trail is located behind the park's Outlaw Trading Post.

Directions: From Gallup, go east on I-40 and get off at Exit 26, which will take you to a frontage road (US 66). Go east on the frontage road for 2 miles, then turn left (north) on NM 566 (there is a sign for Red Rock State Park at this junction). Another 0.5 mile or so will take you to the park's entrance on your left (west).

Acoma Sky City (8)

Located atop a sandstone mesa more than 350 feet above the surrounding terrain, Acoma Pueblo (also known as "Sky City") cuts an imposing figure for the approaching visitor, making obvious its original defensive purpose.

The 70-acre National Historic Landmark features traditional pueblo architecture—adobe structures, *vigas* (wooden beams), and ceremonial kivas—and the massive, two-towered San Esteban del Rey Mission (ca. 1640), the pueblo's most impressive structure.

Sky City can be visited only by taking a guided tour of the pueblo. Because tripod use is not allowed, I recommend setting your ISO to 400 (or higher if necessary) and using shake-reduction lenses or cameras to prevent blurry images. I also suggest taking the earliest tour possible, since the smaller crowds will allow for a more leisurely pace through the village.

One of the first stops will be at San Esteban del Rey Mission, the highlight of the tour. While the guide is explaining the significance of the mission, try to take a little time to visualize a pleasing composition of its façade. When the tour group enters the church, use the opportunity to take your pictures. You might also consider including people in these photos to provide the viewer with a sense of scale. If the day is sunny, use a polarizing filter, but keep in mind you will lose about two stops of light in doing so, risking a blurred shot. No photography is allowed inside the mission or at the cemetery outside its entrance.

Other Sky City photo ops include adobe dwellings, architectural details, and ceremonial kivas, notable for their square size (elsewhere they are round) and bright white ladders piercing New Mexico's brilliant blue sky. You will also have the opportunity to photograph vendors and their crafts, but make sure to ask for permission before photographing them.

Directions: From Albuquerque, drive west on I-40 for 55 miles to Exit 102. Turn left (south) at the exit and follow the signs another 16 miles to the Sky City Cultural Center on your left.

Gallup Inter-Tribal Indian Ceremonial (9)

The Gallup Inter-Tribal Indian Ceremonial is a smorgasbord of Indian culture. During a five-day period in August, the ceremonial hosts a number of very photogenic events such as parades (one during the day, the other at night), beauty contests, rodeos, dancing demonstrations, and my favorite, the pow wows. In addition you will have the opportunity to sample Indian food and browse the many indoor and outdoor booths selling pottery, basketry, rugs, dolls, and other Indian crafts. All this (except for the parades) takes place within the massive sandstone walls of Red Rock State Park about 7 miles east of Gallup. For a detailed schedule of events, visit www.gallupintertribal.com.

Because some of the ceremonial's events are held concurrently, you will have to prioritize what to concentrate on so you don't get overwhelmed by trying to photograph everything. My suggestion is to focus on the pow wows first, then photograph other events as time permits.

Pow wows are iconic of Indian culture in the West and feature colors, textures, and movement that are conducive to great photography. At the ceremonial you will be able to get very close to the action, so a mid-telephoto zoom (up to 300mm or so) will easily yield frame-filling compositions. You might also want to try slow shutter speeds and pan along with the dancers to achieve a pleasingly blurred, painterly effect. Be flexible and move with the action in order to find new and interesting compositions, but pay attention to your backgrounds; uncluttered ones are best. The pow wows that are held late in the afternoon present the best opportunity for flattering light.

The many Indian dancing demonstrations that take place during the ceremonial are also popular with photographers, and they are less crowded than the pow wows. The demonstrations usually feature a small troupe performing a particular dance, such as the Buffalo Dance. Because of the smaller crowds you can get even closer to the action than at the pow wows, though the dances are usually held midday, so bring a flash to fill in the shadows.

If you have time, visit downtown Gallup to photograph the day parade, which features a long line of photo opportunities, including Indian marching bands, dancers, and the Indian Code Talkers float. When the parade moves along a stretch of US 66 ("Route 66"), the challenge here is to find an uncluttered background. However, to give your images a sense of place you might want to include in your background the many weathered "Route 66" signs along the way.

Indian girl dancers, pow wow, Gallup Inter-Tribal Ceremonial

The ceremonial's Indian rodeo is also popular and fun to photograph. For this event set your camera to continuous-shooting mode to capture the fast-moving action. A mid-to-long telephoto zoom (400mm plus) should do the trick here, and be prepared with multiple backup media cards (or plenty of film rolls) to make sure you can keep shooting. Even if you have not photographed a rodeo before, you will soon get the rhythm for when participants are launched into the arena, heads a-bobbing and horses a-bucking. This will allow you to anticipate the action (more or less) and make successful photographs. Try both fast (1/400th second and faster) and slow (around 1/4 second) shutter speeds to freeze and blur the action respectively.

Directions: See the directions for Red Rock State Park, above.

Red Rock Balloon Rally (10)

For three days in early December, about 200 balloonists converge at Red Rock State Park outside Gallup to take to the skies in their float-

ing rainbows. With a backdrop of red sandstone bluffs and deep blue skies, the colorful display offers the photographer almost overwhelming choices. Although the Albuquerque International Balloon Fiesta is a bigger event, the rally's backdrop and opportunities to get close-up views of the balloons are unsurpassed. A complete schedule of events can be found at www.redrockballoonrally.com.

The balloon rally's launch site is adjacent to massive red rock formations, giving you the opportunity to take up-close shots of the pre-flight preparations, as well as the launch itself, against the red sandstone cliffs. For these initial shots, as well as for "landscape" pictures of the balloons flying over the park, use your wide-angle to midrange zoom (24mm–105mm range or so). Lenses 200mm and longer will come in handy for frame-filling compositions of solitary balloons (or small groups) as they drift across the sky.

For a different view of this floating spectacle, photograph the balloons from one of Red Rock Park's two short trails (see entry for Red Rock State Park, above). Both Pyramid Rock Trail and Church Rock Trail offer unique backgrounds for your compositions, including the rocks themselves, deep canyons, and other rock formations. Church Rock Trail is closer to the launch site, while Pyramid Rock Trail is farther away but offers a much higher vantage point. Before heading up either trail, make sure the wind is blowing in the trail's general direction (ask a pilot if you are not sure); otherwise your effort will be for naught. If you have time, it's a good idea to scout the trails the day before to pre-select the best vantage points for your shoot.

Because of the variety of photo possibilities, I recommend spending at least two days photographing the balloon rally. You can concentrate on the more intimate shots one day and on overall compositions on the other.

Directions: See the directions for Red Rock State Park, above.

Totah Festival Indian Market and Pow Wow (11)

Held on two days in September, the Totah Festival Indian Market and Pow Wow includes Indian crafts, a rug auction, and food vendors. However, the main attraction for photographers is the pow wow held each day. Like other pow wows in New Mexico, it features colorful Indian costumes, lively dancing, and traditional Indian songs. Visit www.farmingtonnm.org for a schedule of events.

Because the pow wow is held at 11 AM, the light is likely to be harsh. Bring your flash to fill the shadows in the dancers' faces and costumes, thus bringing out more detail. If the day is overcast, the clouds will act as a giant diffuser and you will not need the flash.

Focus on the dancer's faces (specifically the eyes if possible), since viewers will naturally look there first when looking at your pictures. It's OK if the rest of the image is slightly blurred as this will imply movement and bring life to your pictures. Look for the many small children who participate in the pow wow; they often make compelling subjects because of their unpredictable behavior and cute looks. A mid-telephoto zoom (around 200mm–300mm) will be plenty long to photograph this intimate and fun event.

Directions: From West Broadway (US 64) in downtown Farmington, go north on North Allen Avenue two blocks to West Arrington Street. The Farmington Civic Center is at 200 West Arrington Street (northeast corner of North Allen and West Arrington).

Northwest New Mexico Diversions: Gallup is home to some of the best Indian crafts stores in the Four Corners region, including Richardson's Trading Company right downtown. Shops all over town offer an almost overwhelming variety of crafts, from cheap trinkets to prohibitively expensive rugs, ceramics, and jewelry. Take a stroll around town and see what strikes your fancy. For something to eat, head to the restaurant at the historic El Rancho Hotel on US 66. Despite its faded Western decor, this diner-style restaurant has a loyal following and offers steaks, seafood, and New Mexican fare.

Indian male dancers, pow wow, Totah Festival, Farmington

Adobe façade, door, and flowers; Canyon Road, Santa Fe

II. North Central New Mexico

SEASONAL RATINGS: SPRING ✦✦✦✦ SUMMER ✦✦✦ FALL ✦✦✦✦ WINTER ✦✦

General Description: Much of North Central New Mexico's landscape is dominated by the Rocky Mountains, including the Tusas Mountains west of Taos, the Jemez Mountains west and south of Los Alamos, and the Sangre de Cristo Mountains north and east of Santa Fe, where the Rockies end. But the area is also home to Ghost Ranch, a place favored by American painter Georgia O'Keeffe, where Jurassic sandstone cliffs rise abruptly above the surrounding terrain, reminders of a long-ago era.

North Central New Mexico is also the region's cultural mecca. Santa Fe and Taos lead the way in terms of food and lodging options, galleries, museums, art districts, and cultural events, but the entire area is teeming with small galleries, intimate inns, and roadside vendors selling everything from *ristras* (pepper strings) to jewelry.

Ghost Ranch (12)

Located along the Colorado Plateau's extreme eastern edge, Ghost Ranch features rugged sandstone cliffs reminiscent of Utah's canyon country. Massive rock walls, square-topped bluffs, and blunted spires rise above the surrounding multihued terrain, offering the landscape photographer a variety of opportunities and compositions. The 21,000 acres that comprise Ghost Ranch are owned and operated by the Presbyterian Church, but the ranch's trails are open to the general public.

The best way to photograph at Ghost Ranch is to hike its various (and relatively short) trails. My favorite is the 3-mile (round trip) trail to Chimney Rock, a distinctively shaped sandstone spire. The best time to photograph from the trail is in the morning.

Noted For: Santa Fe and Taos, Georgia O'Keeffe country, mix of Indian and Spanish cultures, pueblo architecture, art and historic districts

Best Times: Spring, early summer, fall, and during listed events

Exertion: Minimal to moderate

Peak Times: Spring: May; summer: June; fall: September; winter: December; during listed events

Facilities: At developed sites

Parking: In lots, on the street, and at trailheads

Sleeps and Eats: Santa Fe, Taos, Los Alamos, Chama

Sites and Events Included: Ghost Ranch, Bandelier National Monument, Santuario de Chimayó, Cumbres & Toltec Scenic Railroad, Eight Northern Indian Pueblos Festival Arts & Crafts Show, Santa Fe Plaza, Palace of the Governors, New Mexico Museum of Art, La Fonda Hotel, Cathedral Basilica of St. Francis of Assisi, Institute of American Indian Arts Museum, Lensic Theater, Loretto Chapel, San Miguel Mission, Santuario de Guadalupe, Canyon Road, Pecos National Historical Park, Aspen Vista Trail, Ravens Ridge Overlook Trail, Burning of Zozobra, Santa Fe Fiesta Entrada, Santa Fe Fiesta Solemn Procession, El Rancho de las Golondrinas Civil War Reenactment, Rodeo de Santa Fe, Christmas Eve Farolito Walk, Taos Pueblo, San Francisco de Asis Church, Rio Grande Gorge Bridge, Rio Grande Gorge Wild Rivers Recreation Area, Taos Pueblo Pow Wow

Chimney Rock, Ghost Ranch

As you climb the uphill but steady trail, you will have varying views of Chimney Rock ahead of you. Look for interesting rocks or colorful hillsides to use as a foreground, and bring a polarizing filter to saturate the blue sky and the rock's red hues. A wide-angle zoom lens will be ideal here, but a mid-telephoto zoom (around 100mm) will come in handy if you wish to take some close-up pictures of the subject. As you reach the top of the mesa you will

Pedernal (9,862 feet) in the distance. Both of these subjects will add interest and context to a close-up shot of Chimney Rock.

If you have time, be sure to explore Ghost Ranch's other trails such as Box Canyon (close-ups of sandstone canyon walls) and Piedra Lumbre (a beautiful open desert hike).

Directions: From Santa Fe, drive north on US 84/285 for about 25 miles to Española. Turn left on US 84 and continue for another 40 miles, through the village of Abiquiu, to the entrance to Ghost Ranch (marked by a sign). Turn right and drive another mile or so to the Ruth Hall Museum of Paleontology (on the left). The marked trailhead for the hike described below is located behind the museum.

Bandelier National Monument (13)

Located on the slopes of the Jemez Mountains, an ancient volcano that erupted about 1 million years ago, Bandelier National Monument combines a landscape of broad mesas and deep canyons with the cultural remains of Ancestral Pueblo peoples who occupied the area about 600 years ago. Several thousand ancient dwellings lie within the 33,000-acre park, but the best known and preserved are found near the visitor center.

Bandelier's main cultural attractions are the numerous ancient dwellings found along Frijoles Canyon, and Alcove House (also known as the Ceremonial Cave), a kiva perched 140 feet above Frijoles Canyon and reached via a series of stone steps and wooden ladders.

From the visitor center, head (roughly) west along Frijoles Canyon on Main Loop Trail, the 2.2-mile (round trip) trail that leads to Alcove House. Soon you will reach the ruins of a small kiva, followed by a great house called Tyuonyi. These ruins are not very impressive from the ground, so keep walking until the trail begins climbing steadily towards Long House, a set of

lose sight of Chimney Rock, but it will appear again, massive and delicate, when you reach the end of the trail. From here you will have spectacular views of the colorful landscape below as well as Abiquiu Reservoir and Cerro

Ladder, reconstructed kiva, Ceremonial Cave, Bandelier National Monument

cliff dwellings on the canyon walls. From the upper section of the trail you will enjoy panoramic views of Tyuonyi below, and in the fall the cottonwoods surrounding the ruins will add some color to your compositions. Long House also provides good close-up views of the cliff dwellings; a wide-angle lens would be ideal here. If the canyon wall is in the sun, put on a polarizer to reduce the reflections caused by the wall's sheen.

After Long House, the trail descends to the canyon floor and continues for another 0.5 mile to Alcove House. A word of warning: although relatively safe, the wooden ladders and stone steps leading to Alcove House are not for folks afraid of heights. If you decide to go up, make sure your backpack and tripod are securely fastened.

Alcove House consists of a ceremonial kiva inside a large alcove, and offers wonderful views of the surrounding canyon. A wooden ladder leads to the inside of the kiva; go inside and take pictures of light shafts entering the sacred structure. The kiva will be in the shade in the morning, a good time to photograph it because contrast will be low. Afternoons are good for inside shots with light streaming in.

Bandelier's trail system also includes Falls Trail, a 4.5-mile (round trip) hike that leads to two small but photogenic waterfalls. These are best photographed in the spring when water levels are high. From the visitor center, follow the signs to Falls Trail, which follows the Frijoles River in a southeasterly direction. The trail is downhill going out and uphill coming back, so plan accordingly. The larger of the two waterfalls, Upper Frijoles Falls, is about 1.5 miles from the visitor center. The smaller waterfall, Lower Frijoles Falls, is about another 0.3 mile down the canyon. If possible, photograph the waterfalls early or late when the canyon is in the shade; this will reduce contrast and make your photographs look better. Use a polarizer to reduce reflections and lengthen your exposures to get that "silky" effect. Both waterfalls are somewhat distant from the trail, so I recommend bringing a lens in the 100mm–200mm range for close-up shots of the falls. A wide-angle lens will allow you to include more of the surrounding rocks and vegetation in your compositions.

Directions: It's approximately 42 miles from Santa Fe to Bandelier's visitor center. From

Santa Fe, drive north on US 84/285 for about 15 miles to Pojoaque. Exit to NM 502 and drive another 11.5 miles to NM 4; follow the signs for Bandelier. Travel west another 12 miles or so on NM 4, through the town of White Rock, to the Bandelier entrance on the left (south) side of the road. The park's visitor center is located 3 miles from the entrance station.

Santuario de Chimayó (14)

Known as "The Lourdes of America" because of the many reported miracles that have taken place at the site, the Santuario de Chimayó (ca. 1816) is a charming, two-tower adobe building with a weathered (and very photogenic) gate at its entrance. Inside, this National Historic Landmark features five beautiful panels of sacred paintings known as *reredos*, though photography is prohibited within the church.

Located in the village of Chimayó in the Sangre de Cristo Mountains, the santuario is easily one of the most visited churches in New Mexico, not only by those seeking a miracle but also by photographers and other artists as well. Every year during Holy Week, thousands of pilgrims walk to Chimayó from as far as Albuquerque to seek a cure or favor.

Get to the Santuario de Chimayó well before sundown (the church photographs best in the afternoon) and walk around the place before you begin photographing it. Although the santuario is battered and worn, you can feel that this is a special place. Slow down a bit and visualize how you'd like to interpret this icon. Think about whether you want to include the adobe entrance in the frame or not; if you do, consider where you would place the entrance in the composition.

Santuario de Chimayó

Architectural photography is a little like portrait photography: your main goal is to flatter the subject as much as possible while keeping it recognizable. This still leaves quite a bit of room for creativity, however. Think about taking a black and white photograph, perhaps adding sepia toning (or another tone) afterwards. Or maybe you want to use an image editing program like Photoshop to make the church look more like a watercolor, or an impressionist painting, or even a stained glass window. Whatever you decide to do, try a number of compositions so you have a wide selection of images when you get down to editing your take.

Directions: Drive north on US 84/285 for about 16 miles (through Pojoaque) and turn right (east) on NM 503. Go another 8 miles to NM 98 and turn left (north). An additional 3 miles will take you to the village of Chimayó. The santuario will be on your right. Follow the signs to its parking lot.

Cumbres & Toltec Scenic Railroad (15)

Completed in 1880, the Cumbres & Toltec Scenic Railroad offers a truly authentic "frontier west" ride on a steam locomotive through the high, forested meadows of the Rocky Mountains straddling the New Mexico and Colorado borders. Highlights of the 64-mile

Cumbres & Toltec Railroad and fall colors near Chama

journey include the Chama depot, Toltec Gorge, Windy Point (the highest railroad summit in the West), tunnels, and trestles.

The Cumbres & Toltec's Chama train depot is the best place to begin your photo shoot. Get there early to take pictures of the station's main building, the boarding platform, the water tower, and the steam locomotive getting ready for departure. Numerous other cars also make for interesting photo subjects, and don't forget the engineers and other train staff, as they will add human interest to your pictures. Once under way, your challenge will be to make quality photographs from a moving train, not easy in these old locomotives. Use shake-reduction lenses or camera bodies if you have them, and ratchet your ISO to 400 (or higher if needed) to insure that your images are sharp. Although you will have plenty of opportunities to photograph landscapes during the journey, you might want to focus on images that include the train in the landscape. You came to photograph the train, after all, and the late-morning departure means the light will not be ideal for landscape photography anyway.

My favorite way to photograph the train, however, is from the numerous access points along NM 17 (or CO 17), rather than while riding the train itself. You will have to do a little scouting beforehand and calculate the times the train will pass by a particular spot, but your images, especially in the fall when the aspens and cottonwoods turn yellow, will benefit from including the railroad in its beautiful context. One of the most popular spots from which to photograph the Cumbres & Toltec is "Kodak Rock" (mile post 331.2), where you can view the train as it winds around Windy Pass above. Another good location is at the NM 17 crossing (mile post 343.2), which offers good coming and going-away photo opportunities. For a thorough list of photo-worthy vantage points, visit www.chamachoochoo.com and click on "Cumbres Toltec Information."

Directions: From Santa Fe, drive north on US 84/285 for about 25 miles to Española. Turn left on US 84 and continue all the way to Chama. Total distance is about 105 miles.

Eight Northern Indian Pueblos Festival Arts & Crafts Show (16)

The Eight Northern Indian Pueblos Festival Arts & Crafts Show, a Northern New Mexico tradition since 1971, features pueblo dances, Indian arts and crafts, and traditional pueblo food like *posole* (a hearty soup of corn and pork or chicken), bowls of red or green chile, and freshly baked oven bread. Organized and operated by Native Americans, this event has an authentic feel that is often not found in other festivals.

The most photogenic events of the festival are the traditional pueblo dances. Although the festival is popular, it is easy to find a good vantage point to photograph the action, especially if you move around following the dancers. I recommend a lens in the 200mm–300mm range to get frame-filling compositions, though a wider angle zoom will also come in handy to include the crowd enjoying the festivities. The Eagle Dance is my favorite, as dancers, bedecked in colorful feathers and eagle-head masks, swing their arms in imitation of an eagle in flight. Especially endearing are the small children who take part in the dance, still a little clumsy but focused and earnest just the same. Another favorite is the Buffalo Dance, where participants wear buffalo heads and shuffle, backs curved and heads down, around the arena.

To round out your image collection of the event, don't forget to photograph some of the beautiful ceramics, sculptures, and other crafts on display, but as always ask each artisan before taking any photographs.

Directions: From Santa Fe, drive north on US 84/285 for about 25 miles to Española. In Española turn right on NM 86 as you go through town. The Eight Northern Pueblos visitor center is about 2 miles north of Española on your right.

Eagle Dance, San Juan Pueblo, Eight Northern Indian Pueblos Festival Arts & Crafts Show

Santa Fe Center

Founded by Spanish settlers in 1610, Santa Fe is one of the oldest cities in the United States. Today as then, the town's physical and cultural center is its leafy plaza, surrounded by shops, restaurants, hotels, galleries, museums, and churches. Many of the buildings on or near the plaza offer great photo opportunities to those who enjoy photographing historic structures. Although many of the buildings are magnificent examples of traditional adobe architecture, you will find some interesting surprises along the way. The following is a suggested walking tour of some of the most photogenic spots and buildings in Santa Fe's core.

Shaded by large cottonwood trees and perennially busy, the **Santa Fe Plaza (17)**, with its many benches and a gazebo, photographs well almost any time of the year, especially if you like people photography. Here you will find Indian vendors, tourists, and locals mixing it up as they go about their business. My favorite time to photograph people in the plaza is during fall, when the yellow cottonwoods provide a colorful canopy to the activity below. I also recommend photographing around the plaza during special events such as the Santa Fe Fiesta's Entrada, where conquistador reenactors on horseback portray the Spaniards' entrance into the city in 1692 (see entry for the Entrada below).

Located on the north side of the plaza, the **Palace of the Governors (18)** (1610) epitomizes the archetypical adobe structure of the region, featuring bulky adobe walls, *vigas* (wood beams) sticking out of the roof, and a large portal to shade passersby from the desert sun. Although the palace is architecturally rather plain, it comes to life every day of the year (rain or shine or snow) as Native American artisans line up shoulder to shoulder under the portal to offer their wares to eager tourists.

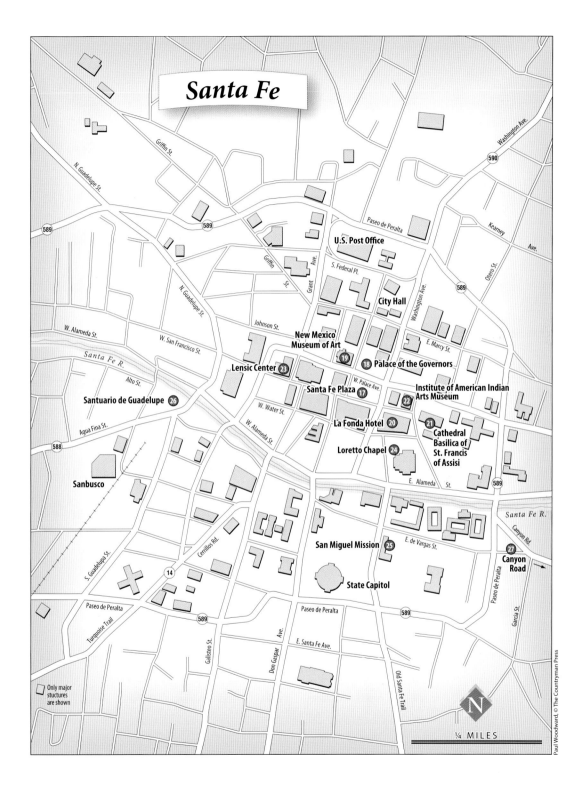

Santa Fe

Griffin St.

N. Guadelupe St.

589

590

Washington Ave.

Kearney Ave.

Otero St.

Paseo de Peralta

U.S. Post Office

S. Federal Pl.

Grant Ave.

Griffin St.

N. Guadelupe St.

City Hall

Washington Ave.

589

Johnson St.

W. Alameda St.

W. San Francisco St.

Santa Fe R.

Alto St.

New Mexico Museum of Art

E. Marcy St.

19

Lensic Center 23

18 **Palace of the Governors**

Santuario de Guadalupe 26

Agua Fina St.

588

W. Palace Ave.

Santa Fe Plaza 17

Institute of American Indian Arts Museum

22

W. Water St.

W. Alameda St.

La Fonda Hotel 20

21

Loretto Chapel 24

Cathedral Basilica of St. Francis of Assisi

Sanbusco

E. Alameda St.

589

Santa Fe R.

Canyon Rd.

Cerrillos Rd.

S. Guadelupe St.

San Miguel Mission 25

E. de Vargas St.

27 **Canyon Road**

14

State Capitol

Paseo de Peralta

589

Paseo de Peralta

Paseo de Peralta

589

Garcia St.

Turquoise Trail

Galisteo St.

Don Gaspar Ave.

E. Santa Fe Ave.

Old Santa Fe Trail

Only major stuctures are shown

N

¼ MILES

Paul Woodward, © The Countryman Press

Santa Fe Plaza in the fall; Palace of the Governors in background

Be there early or late to avoid the harsh light of midday, and photograph the activity from either end of the building to show the organized chaos of shoppers bargaining with vendors over the price of jewelry, pottery, weavings, and other crafts. Include the *vigas* in your compositions to get a sense of place and give your images context.

Across the street and just west of the Palace of the Governors, the **New Mexico Museum of Art (19)** is a superb example of Pueblo revival architecture, now commonly known as "Santa Fe style." Inaugurated in 1917, the museum's entrance resembles a Spanish mission, complete with two bell towers, large wooden doors, massive adobe walls, and *vigas*. The museum's mud-colored adobe walls and towers photograph beautifully in late afternoon, when the sun's low rays cover the structure in warm light. Because space is a little tight around the building, use a wide-angle lens to photograph the museum's impressive façade. For dramatic compositions, consider getting under one of the towers and shooting upwards against the bright blue New Mexico skies (use a polarizer to increase contrast and saturation). A lens in the 100mm area will allow you to take pictures of details like doors, windows, and *vigas* casting shadows against the walls.

Since the city's founding in the early 1600s, there has been a fonda (inn) off the Santa Fe Plaza's southeast corner. Today that spot is occupied by **La Fonda (20)**, a Pueblo revival hotel built in 1921 and brimming with charm. La Fonda comes to life during the Christmas season, where the building's parapets are decorated with hundreds of farolitos (formerly candles inside paper bags, but more recently modern electrical lights designed to look like the original) and a full-size manger scene. Visit La Fonda at twilight and photograph its exterior as the Christmas decorations are first turned on. You will need a wide-angle lens to get it all in, but bring longer lenses (100mm or so) to also capture some of the holiday details individually.

Christmas or not, La Fonda's interiors are a fun place to photograph, especially if the weather outside is uncooperative. The hotel's interior architecture features large beams, carved corbels, and balconies. The lobby, hallways, and restaurant are decorated with paintings, stained glass, tin and copper light fixtures, hand-painted tiles, woodcarvings, and other crafts by local artisans, giving the hotel a kitschy but irresistible ambiance. Walk up to the hotel's second level, where you can view and photograph colorful La Plazuela Restaurant, designed to resemble an open plaza setting. Use long shutter speeds of 1/4 second and longer to blur the movement of the restaurant's patrons and staff, which will make for a dynamic

The New Mexico Museum of Art, Santa Fe

photograph and capture the place's high energy.

A block east of the plaza on San Francisco Street is the **Cathedral Basilica of St. Francis of Assisi (21)**, the town's grandest religious structure. Built between 1869 and 1886 by Archbishop Jean-Baptiste Lamy, the French-designed Romanesque revival building is an anomaly among the city's more traditional adobe structures. The cathedral faces west, so its imposing façade—consisting of two bell towers, a large arched door, and a rose (stained glass) window—photographs beautifully in late afternoon. A wide-angle zoom lens will come in handy because you will be photographing in tight quarters. You might also photograph the cathedral straight on from San Francisco Street using a longer lens, but be careful with distracting elements like lampposts, traffic signs, and overhead wires. My favorite time to photograph the cathedral is at twilight, as the building is illuminated by large floodlights and stands out against the intense navy blue sky just before total darkness.

The cathedral's interior is a good place to photograph when conditions outside are not conducive to shooting. In addition to the traditional shots (the church's nave and stained glass windows), look for the wooden statue of Our Lady of Peace (ca. early 1600s), the oldest

St. Francis Cathedral, Santa Fe

representation of the Madonna in the U.S. Known locally as *La Conquistadora,* the three-foot statue is clad in elaborate dresses made by local artisans. *La Conquistadora* can also be seen and photographed outside during certain feasts; see the entry for the Santa Fe Fiesta Solemn Procession, for example.

Across the street from the cathedral is the **Institute of American Indian Arts Museum (22)**, a Pueblo revival building listed in the National Register of Historic Places. The museum has a shady portal with large posts holding it up, two towers, and a second-floor balcony. The building faces east so it photographs well in the morning. A good spot from which to photograph the IAIA is from the small plaza located in front of the cathedral's main entrance, since it's elevated and offers a good overall perspective of the museum. Also, look for graphic shots showing vigas or posts as they cast their shadows on brightly lit walls or walkways.

Located a few blocks west of the cathedral on San Francisco Street, the **Lensic Theater (23)** is one of the most unusual buildings in Santa Fe. Built in 1931 in what has been described as pseudo-Moorish, Spanish Renaissance style, the Lensic combines plain adobe construction with elaborate architectural details such as arched windows and carved dragons along the top of the structure. The building faces roughly south and photographs well in the morning, when the sun illuminates its east side along Burro Alley. The front/east side of the theater offers good views of the theater's side and façade, including its old-fashioned marquee. Consider using your longer lenses (120mm or longer) to capture some of the theater's architectural details.

Loretto Chapel (24) is located on Old Santa Fe Trail just south of La Fonda. Modeled after the Sainte-Chapelle in Paris and built in 1873 by the Sisters of Loretto, this Gothic-

Lensic Theater, Santa Fe

style architectural jewel is currently a popular museum. The chapel is best known for its spiral staircase, constructed without nails, center post, or other visible means of support. According to legend, the staircase was built by a mysterious carpenter called Joseph, who some believe was St. Joseph himself.

The chapel's stone construction features elaborate architectural details around its façade, a rose (stained glass) window, square buttresses, and spires reaching for the sky. The chapel's entrance faces west, so the best time to photograph it is late afternoon. Space in

"Miraculous" stairs, Loretto Chapel, Santa Fe

Photograph the staircase first, before the crowds arrive, then work on other shots. The staircase can be photographed up close, showing its intricate woodwork; from afar, showing it in context; and by including only a portion of its surroundings such as stained glass windows. The church's altar, stained glass windows, and religious icons also make for interesting subjects. There is a small entrance fee.

Built in the early 17th century, **San Miguel Mission (25)** is one of the oldest churches in the United States. Located about two blocks south of the Loretto Chapel on Old Santa Fe Trail, the church is a simple adobe structure featuring massive walls and a single bell tower. The mission's façade faces west, making it an ideal location for a late afternoon shoot. Try photographing the mission from its left side to include the large stone buttresses that hold up the structure. Inside, the mission features simple wooden pews and floors, the San Jose Bell (reportedly dating to 1356), a beautiful hand-painted *reredo* (screen behind the altar), and other religious art. Tripods are allowed inside. There is a small entrance fee.

Believed to be the oldest shrine in the United States honoring the Virgin of Guadalupe, the **Santuario de Guadalupe (26)** (ca. 1800) is located about four blocks west of the plaza on Guadalupe Street. The adobe church features a simple façade topped by a bell tower and a red tile roof. The east-facing façade makes the church a good photo subject for early morning. Be careful when composing wide-angle shots, since there are a number of power lines and cables in front. A good choice for an establishing shot is to walk across the street and use a longer lens for a tight composition. This will have the added bonus of avoiding the "falling back" look that often occurs when photographing architectural subjects with a wide-angle lens looking up. In the fall, you can use yellow chamisa shrubs (also

front of the church is limited, so use a wide-angle lens for your overall shot.

The chapel's main attraction is its spiral staircase. Tripods are allowed but they can be hard to deploy if the interior is crowded; I therefore suggest getting there as early as possible (visit www.lorettochapel.com for hours).

Santuario de Guadalupe Church, Santa Fe

known as rubber rabbitbrush) as a strong, colorful foreground for your compositions.

The church's interior, though simple, does offer some photo opportunities, including hand-carved religious figures called *santos,* a 1783 painting of the Virgin of Guadalupe, and a traditional New Mexican carved and painted altar screen. Today the church houses a museum, and donations are accepted. Tripods are allowed inside.

Canyon Road (27), the last entry in Santa Fe's walking photo tour, is the city's main art district. Named one of America's Ten Great Streets by the American Planning Association in 2007, Canyon Road features a collection of over a hundred art galleries and studios, one-of-a-kind shops, world-class restaurants, and historic adobe residences. This eclectic combination makes Canyon Road a fun place to photograph. The road is accessed from Paseo de Peralta near West Alameda Avenue.

One of the most popular subjects to photograph in Canyon Road is doors, which come in a variety of colors, shapes, and textures. In summer many of the doors can be photographed above colorful flowers planted by home and gallery owners. Look for unique doors with iron hardware such as knockers or grates, or for weathered doors with texture and character. Follow the many narrow alleys that lead from Canyon Road and see what you can find. Remember, however, that some of the doors along the road lead to privately owned homes, so be sensitive to their privacy.

Other subjects along Canyon Road that will be of interest to photographers include architectural details of historic buildings (windows, *vigas, ristras*), colorful mailboxes (you will have to hunt for these), public art (but remember that copyright laws will have a bearing on how you can use these), gardens (in season), and the road itself as it meanders away from you. And if you are in Santa Fe during Christ-mas, do not miss Canyon Road's Farolito Walk on Christmas Eve (see entry for Christmas Eve Farolito Walk, below).

Directions: Santa Fe is located about 65 miles northeast of Albuquerque off I-25. To reach the plaza, get off at Exit 282 going north on St. Francis Drive (US 84/285). Drive an additional 4 miles or so to West Alameda Avenue and turn right (east). Turn left (north) at Sandoval Street, then right (east) at West San Francisco. There's a parking structure on your right. When you leave the parking structure, turn right (east) on West San Francisco. The plaza will be three blocks down on your left. If you are staying in Santa Fe, ask the hotel staff for the best way to get to the plaza.

Santa Fe Environs

Pecos National Historical Park (28)

Pecos National Historical Park contains the ruins of a large Indian pueblo and Spanish missions. Originally settled by the Pecos Indians in the 1400s, the village quickly became an important trading center in the southern Sangre de Cristo Mountains. In the late 1500s Spanish *conquistadores* appeared on the scene to stay, and by 1620 Franciscan monks had established a church and a convent in the village.

An easy 1.25-mile loop trail will take you to the pueblo ruins and the hulking remains of what was once one of the most impressive missions north of Mexico City, Nuestra Señora de los Angeles de Porciuncula. A beautifully reconstructed kiva along the trail, complete with a wooden ladder, makes for a perfect foreground to photograph the mission in the distance. Use a wide-angle lens for this shot and get low to the ground to emphasize the round kiva. Because the mission and pueblo ruins are plain and mud-colored, look for interesting cloud formations to add interest to your compositions. And as always, don't forget to look for architectural details like *vigas* and weathered entryways to round out your image collection.

Directions: From Santa Fe, drive 25 miles on I-25 north to Exit 299, and continue on NM 50 to Pecos Village. Turn right (south) on NM 63 and travel another 2 miles to the park.

Aspen Vista Trail (29)

One of the most popular hikes in the Sangre de Cristo Mountains, Aspen Vista Trail features large aspen stands that turn bright yellow in the fall. Along the way, the moderate trail also offers panoramic views of Santa Fe below. The well-graded trail is almost 6 miles one way, but the nicest views can be reached within a mile or so from the trailhead.

Fall is the best time to photograph the aspen trees and landscapes along Aspen Vista Trail. Although difficult to predict, peak color typically occurs the first part of October. Both mornings and afternoons offer excellent opportunities for fall-color photography, but I prefer the mornings because of smaller crowds and subdued winds. Aspen leaves attain that special yellow glow when the sun is behind them, so getting up before dawn is not critical for good results.

Before starting your hike, take in the broad views of the aspen forest right below you. In addition to grand landscape compositions, try

Ruined adobe walls at sunset, Pecos National Historical Park

using a telephoto lens 200mm or longer to make more intimate images of particularly appealing sections of trees. As you begin to hike up the trail, you will be very close to the trees, so consider taking tight shots of aspen tree trunks with out-of-focus, shimmering leaves in the background. Try horizontal and vertical compositions to give variety to your shot. For compositions that include the sky, use a polarizer filter to increase color saturation; you will love the look of the shining yellow aspen leaves against the intense blue skies. If you are feeling playful and artistic, try some hand-held shots where you purposely pan the camera up and down. Try different shutter speeds and panning motions to see what you like best.

At about a mile you will come to an overlook with an expansive view of aspen stands below. This is a good spot to have a snack and turn around.

Directions: From Santa Fe, take Washington Avenue north from Paseo de Peralta 0.1 mile to Artist Road/NM 475. Turn right and continue for another 13 miles towards the Santa Fe Ski Area. The trailhead will be on your right.

Ravens Ridge Overlook Trail (30)

Located within the Santa Fe National Forest, the Ravens Ridge Overlook is only minutes from the Santa Fe Plaza. This steep but short trail (1.5 miles one way) offers spectacular

Artistic rendering of aspens in fall colors, from Aspen Vista Trail

Snow covered trees and Santa Fe Baldy from Ravens Ridge Trail, Santa Fe National Forest

summit views and an opportunity for grand landscape photography. From the overlook you will see beautiful aspen stands below you and mighty Santa Fe Baldy (12,622 feet) to the north.

From the information kiosk, follow Winsor Trail 254 uphill towards Lake Katherine. As you ascend a series of switchbacks, look for pockets of aspen stands that make great photo subjects in the fall. About 0.5 mile into the hike you will reach a clearing and a fence marking the entrance to the Pecos Wilderness Area. This is another good spot to make intimate pictures of aspen trees in fall. Turn right (uphill) before entering the wilderness area and follow an unmarked (but well-trodden) trail parallel to a fence. About 1.5 miles from the trailhead you will reach the overlook.

Fall is one of the best times to photograph from the overlook, as temperatures will be cooler and the changing aspen trees will add color to your landscapes. My favorite time to photograph here, however, is winter, especially after a heavy blanket of fresh snow has covered Santa Fe Baldy and everything else. For this excursion you will need snowshoes and probably a flask of hot chocolate, but the effort will be worth it. Bring your polarizer filter to increase color saturation in the sky, and your wide-angle zoom for your grand landscapes. Include some nearby trees in the foreground to frame your image and provide some scale. Whether you visit in fall or winter, bring a zoom in the 100mm–200mm range to take tight pictures of the aspen trunks in the area.

Directions: From Santa Fe, take Washington

Avenue north from Paseo de Peralta 0.1 mile to Artist Road/NM 475. Turn right and continue for another 14 miles to the Santa Fe Ski Area. Park at the Winsor Trailhead on the northwest corner of the lot near an information kiosk.

Santa Fe Events

Santa Fe Fiesta

First celebrated in 1712, the Santa Fe Fiesta is the oldest community celebration in the United States. Held each year in September, the Fiesta's many events range from the exuberant to the solemn, from the artistic to the kitschy. Below I describe three of my favorite events to photograph. For a detailed schedule, visit www.santafefiesta.org.

A relative newcomer to the Fiesta, the first **Burning of Zozobra (31)** took place in 1924, when Santa Fe artist Will Shuster created a large (49 feet tall), hideous marionette, also known as "Old Man Gloom," to be burned "to dispel the travails and hardships of the previous year," as described in the event's website. Although fun to photograph, keep in mind that this event is a wild one, with over 20,000 people typically in attendance and little room to maneuver. Get there early to scout the area and get a good vantage point, and bring a tripod because you will be shooting in low light conditions. Begin photographing the marionette before the burning, using people in the foreground to add scale to your compositions. Right before the burning begins, the park's lights will be turned off.

The marionette's arms, head, and mouth actually move, so some of your shots will be blurred, illustrating the chaotic atmosphere of this madcap celebration. Keep shooting

Zozobra—"Old Man Gloom"—and fire dancers, Santa Fe Fiesta

through the few minutes it takes for Zozobra to burn to the ground, using a wide-angle lens to capture establishing shots, and longer lenses (in the 100mm–200mm range) to get close-ups of Old Man Gloom's last moments.

The **Entrada (32)**, literally "entrance" or "entry" in Spanish, recreates the peaceful return of the Spanish to Santa Fe in 1692, after they had fled in the Pueblo Revolt of 1680. The event features a reenactment of Diego de Vargas leading his horse-mounted conquistadores in a triumphant entrance into town, with the original woodcarved statue of the Virgin Mary known as La Conquistadora.

Carefully note the sun's position and different backgrounds when you first arrive at the plaza. You want to avoid shooting into the sun because of lens flare, and ideally your background should add to the composition (out-of-focus adobe buildings instead of power lines and poles). Set up your camera to a high ISO (at least 400) and use a shake-reduction lens if you have one, since you will be moving around and shooting hand-held to photograph the entrance. A mid-telephoto lens in the 28mm–135mm range will be most useful, although a longer lens will come in handy for frame-filling shots of the conquistadores and *La Conquistadora*. Remember to take vertical compositions as well as horizontal ones.

Also held around the plaza, the **Solemn Procession (33)** has the reverent, subdued feel one would expect of a religious ceremony. The procession features the conquistadores, this time on foot and with their helmets under their arms to show respect; padres and attendants carrying crosses and incense; a contingent of Indian Buffalo Dancers; *señoritas* in traditional Spanish dresses; and *La Conquistadora*. Bringing up the rear is the current Archbishop of Santa Fe and his attendants. It all ends with a slow entrance into the cathedral.

Spanish "conquistador" on horseback, Santa Fe Fiesta

Once again it is important to watch your backgrounds to avoid clutter and distractions. An f-stop of 5.6 will be helpful in blurring the background so that it does not distract from your subjects. The slow pace of the procession is ideal for moving around looking for pleasing compositions. You might want to first take establishing shots showing the procession making its way around the plaza, then work on detail shots showing *La Conquistadora*, the incense-carrying attendants, the Buffalo Dancers and so on. I also like to include a shot of the procession heading into the cathedral.

Directions: Fort Marcy Park, the venue for the Burning of Zozobra, is within walking distance of town; walk north on Old Taos Highway for a few blocks and the park will be on your right (just follow the crowds). Parking is very limited at the park and not recommended. Both

Confederate army soldier, Civil War reenactment, Rancho de las Golondrinas Living History Museum, Santa Fe

the Entrada and the Solemn Procession are held in the plaza in the center of town.

El Rancho de las Golondrinas Civil War Reenactment (34)

Located on 200 acres in a farming valley just south of Santa Fe, El Rancho de las Golondrinas is a living history museum dedicated to the heritage and culture of Spanish colonial New Mexico. The museum offers visitors the opportunity to experience, through reenactors dressed in period clothing, what life was like during colonial times. The ranch's structures include a schoolhouse, churches, barns, a blacksmith shop, mills, and many other historical buildings. Throughout the year, the museum hosts a number of special events, such as a Civil War reenactment (held in May), complete with a military band, cannon fire, and full-out battles.

Before going to the museum, double-check the schedule of events to make sure you get the most out of your visit (www.golondrinas.org). Typically there will be a military band playing near the entrance to the ranch; soldiers' encampments featuring period tents, cooking fires, and soldiers getting ready for battle; and other soldiers conducting drills, some of them on horses. Bring a tripod to photograph the many historical buildings in the ranch, but be prepared for rapid-fire, handheld photography once the battle begins.

Civil War reenactors are typically very friendly and more than happy to pose for photographs, so make sure you get some semi-formal environmental portraits before the action begins. Although the soldiers do not mind photographers and other spectators being close to the action, stay clear from the front of cannon and other weapons; they are very loud when discharged and can cause ear damage. If in doubt, ask any of the soldiers and they will instruct you as to what distance you should keep.

Once the battle begins you will have the opportunity to photograph infantry brigades going at it on ridges and around buildings, as well as cavalry units lining up in open fields. There will also be a fife and drum unit near (but off) the battlefield, providing background music (and photo ops) to the entire affair. It is relatively easy to get close to the infantry brigades as they engage each other in the field, so a mid-telephoto zoom in the 28mm–180mm range will be useful here. For close-up shots of soldiers, or for photographing the cavalry in the field, I suggest using 200mm lenses or longer. Make sure you have enough space in your memory cards because there will be plenty to photograph.

Directions: From Santa Fe, take I-25 Exit 276; from Albuquerque, take I-25 Exit 276B. Go north (right) on NM 599, then turn left at the light on West Frontage Road. About 0.5 mile from NM 599, turn right on Los Pinos Road. The museum is another 3.2 miles on the left side of the road.

Rodeo de Santa Fe (35)

First held in 1949, the Rodeo de Santa Fe is a Professional Rodeo Cowboys Association (PRCA)–sponsored event, and as such features all the traditional competitions like individual and team roping, barrel racing, saddle and bareback bronc riding, and bull riding. The event also includes a mutton-busting contest for kids, a carnival midway, concession stands, and vendors of western gear and apparel. The rodeo is held in late June (Wednesday through Satur-

Cowboy on bucking horse, bareback riding competition, Rodeo de Santa Fe

day). Visit www.rodeodesantafe.org for more information and a complete schedule of events.

To get the best possible shots of the rodeo, it's important to get a front row seat. This will allow you to kneel near the fence without interfering with other spectators' view of the arena. Bring your long zoom lenses (200mm and longer) to get close-up images of the riders and

Farolitos and Chiaroscuro Gallery with Christmas lights, Canyon Road, Christmas Eve Farolito Walk, Santa Fe

their mounts, and be prepared to shoot hand-held as the action is fast and furious. Use a high ISO (at least 400) and shutter speeds (1/500th second and higher) to freeze the action, but try slower speeds and a panning motion for blurred shots showing motion and excitement. Because the rodeo will start before dusk, you will be able to get sharp images earlier during your shoot. As it gets darker, it will become harder to freeze the action, so go with the flow and experiment with blurred shots then.

If possible, consider leaving your seat and visiting the arena's pens, where you can photograph the cowboys getting ready to mount their animals, the actual mounting, and the violent release. A wide-angle lens would be ideal here to show both the cowboy and his surroundings. Also consider using the wide-angle lens to take establishing shots of the crowd in the foreground and the arena beyond. This type of shot will be most effective from the top of the grandstand. To complete your collection, browse through the many vendors' booths and take detail pictures of saddles, leather belts, hats, and other Western gear.

Directions: From Santa Fe drive south on St. Francis (US 84/285). Turn right on Zia Road, which turns into Rodeo Road. From Rodeo Road, turn right onto Richards Avenue. The entrance to the rodeo is on the right.

Christmas Eve Farolito Walk (36)

For over 30 years Canyon Road, Santa Fe's most exclusive gallery address, has hosted a Christmas Eve stroll. Businesses and private homes along the road are decorated with Christmas ornaments, traditional lights, and thousands of *farolitos* (votive candles in paper bags). During the evening many shops and galleries offer walkers *bizcochitos* (anise-flavored cookies) as well as hot chocolate and cider, and small bonfires help strollers stay warm.

Arrive early to take photographs while the

skies are a rich, cobalt blue; by getting there early you will also avoid the biggest crowds. Bring your tripod since you'll be photographing in low light conditions. Use a wide-angle zoom in the 18mm–35mm range to photograph strollers walking amid the holiday lights. A longer lens will come in handy when photographing details such as doors, buildings, close-ups of *farolitos,* and so on. Be careful with including too much sky after it becomes black; dark areas tend to show a lot of noise in your images, especially at ISO 400 or higher. If your camera has a noise reduction feature, engage it, but keep in mind this will increase your download times.

To tell a story with your pictures, consider including families, carolers, and other strollers in your compositions, especially when they are close to bonfires or other warm light sources. The soft glow of the fire will flatter your human subjects. Because of the low light conditions and long exposures, most people in your images will be blurred. This will add a magical, ethereal feel to your Christmas Eve pictures.

Directions: The beginning of Canyon Road is off Paseo de Peralta, just south of its intersection with East Alameda Street.

Taos

Taos Pueblo (37)

Continuously inhabited for over a thousand years, Taos Pueblo is the only living Native American community designated as both a UN-ESCO World Heritage Site and a National Historic Landmark. Currently, approximately 150 people live within the town. The pueblo features multi-tiered adobe dwellings, ceremonial kivas, a cemetery, and the San Geronimo Catholic Church, all backed up by the Sangre de Cristo Mountains. During visiting hours, a number of shops sell traditional Taos pueblo crafts such as pottery, drums, and silver jewelry.

San Geronimo Church, Taos Pueblo

Morning is the best time to visit and photograph Taos Pueblo. Not only will the crowds be lighter, but the sun will illuminate the face of San Geronimo Church as well as many of the adobe structures. Tripods are not allowed in the pueblo, so set your ISO to 400 or higher and use shake-reduction technology if you have it.

Use a wide-angle zoom in the 18mm–35mm

San Francisco de Asis Church, St. Francis statue and reflection, Taos

and the cross-topped entrance to the walls surrounding the church.

If you wish to photograph pueblo residents or their crafts, ask their permission first. If you encounter a willing subject, consider taking both a portrait photograph as well as an environmental image showing the subject in his or her surroundings.

Directions: From Santa Fe, drive north on US 84/285 to Española, then follow NM 68 northeast to Taos. Taos Pueblo is just north of modern Taos. Driving distance from Santa Fe is about 72 miles.

San Francisco de Asis Church (38)

Completed in 1815, the San Francisco de Asis Church is easily one of the most photographed missions in the Southwest, and its massive adobe structure has been memorialized by numerous artists, such as painter Georgia O'Keeffe and photographer Ansel Adams. The Spanish colonial building features twin bell towers, an arched entryway, and a courtyard surrounding the entrance. Inside the courtyard there is a statue of St. Francis of Assisi, the church's namesake. Most notable, however, is the church's modern, cubist-like back, often interpreted in a semi-abstract manner.

The front of the church faces east, so it photographs best in the morning. You will need a wide-angle zoom in the 18mm–35mm range to photograph the courtyard, the church's façade, and its commanding bell towers. Consider including the courtyard's cross-topped entrance in the foreground with the church in the background, or even showing the façade framed by the entrance (you'll have to get low to the ground for this shot). Don't forget to take pictures of the façade at an angle to show the church's massive adobe buttresses and give your images depth. You might also want to include the statue of St. Francis in some of your

range to take overall shots of the dwellings and surrounding mountains. A longer lens (100mm and longer) will work well for taking close-up shots of adobe ovens, windows, and doors. When photographing the church, make sure to take pictures of the entire structure as well as architectural details like crosses, bell towers,

compositions. As usual when photographing architecture, use a tripod for tack-sharp images.

Come back in the afternoon to photograph the mission's back. Unfortunately, vehicles in the parking lot and power lines and poles will interfere with some compositions, so look for ways to avoid these distractions by taking tight shots of the structure. As an alternative, erase unwanted elements after capture using editing software. However, if your goal is to license your pictures, I recommend disclosing any heavy manipulation of your images to potential clients.

Directions: From Taos, drive south on NM 68 for about 4 miles. The back of the church (and a small parking area) will be on the left after crossing NM 518.

Rio Grande Gorge Bridge (39)

In 1966, the year after it was built, the Rio Grande Gorge Bridge was named Most Beautiful Bridge in the "long span" category by the American Institute of Steel Construction. Spanning 1,280 feet across the Rio Grande, the bridge towers 650 feet above the river and is the second highest in the country. The continuous steel deck structure features two 300-foot approach spans and a 600-foot center span, giving the bridge a symmetrical, photogenic appearance. The bridge is located above one of the most impressive sections of the Rio Grande Gorge.

Because the Rio Grande runs in a north/south direction at the bridge, either early morning or late afternoon will work well for photographing the span. A hiking trail starts at the rest area and heads south along the west side of the gorge. Within the first mile of the flat, easy trail, you will encounter a number of great spots to photograph the bridge straddling the gorge. Sage brushes, desert grasses, and rocky escarpments provide a variety of foregrounds for your wide-angle compositions. Also bring your longer zoom lenses for more intimate renditions of the bridge.

Especially during cloudless days, bring your split neutral density filters to reduce the contrast between the shaded side of the gorge and the sky. A tripod will be essential for tack-sharp images of the bridge and the surrounding landscape.

Rio Grande Gorge and Bridge, near Taos

Directions: From Taos, drive north on NM 68 for 5 miles to its intersection with US 64. Turn left (west) on US 64 and drive another 7 miles to the bridge. Cross the bridge and park in the rest area parking lot on your left.

Rio Grande Gorge Wild Rivers Recreation Area (40)

Administered by the Bureau of Land Management, the Wild Rivers Recreation Area has been set aside to protect a portion of the 68-mile-long Rio Grande Gorge, and specifically the confluence of the Rio Grande and Red River. This rugged area north of Taos features an 800-foot deep volcanic canyon carved by the Rio Grande, sagebrush and piñon-covered flatlands, and ancient juniper forests.

The Wild Rivers Recreation Area offers two photographic vantage points: the rim above the river, and river level. From either location you will need a wide-angle lens to capture the expansive vistas, and a sturdy tripod to steady your camera while using small apertures (at least f16).

River and bluffs, Rio Grande Gorge Wild Rivers Recreation Area

Probably the most spectacular rim-top vantage point is the La Junta Overlook at the end of the road, which offers aerial views of the confluence of the Rio Grande and Red River. Coming in a close second in terms of grand vistas, the Chiflo Recreation Site (not an official "overlook") is also an option, especially at first light when the sun rakes across the mesa tops and starts to peek into the deep canyon.

For more intimate (though no less grand) views of the Rio Grande, you will have to put on your hiking boots and walk to river level. From the La Junta Overlook, the 1.2-mile (one way) moderate-to-difficult La Junta Trail drops 800 feet to the river. Walk along the river on River Trail to find a pleasing composition. Use a polarizer filter to slow down your shutter speeds and give the rushing water a silky appearance. Get low to the ground and use large boulders in the foreground to anchor your compositions. Another good access point to the river is from the Chiflo Recreation Site, which offers a more civilized, 0.5-mile hike (one way) to the water 320 feet below.

Directions: From Taos, drive north on NM 522 about 23 miles. Turn left (west) on NM 378. Another 12 miles will take you to the La Junta Overlook and the end of the road.

Taos Pueblo Pow Wow (41)

Attracting participants from all over North America, the Taos Pueblo Pow Wow is both a dance competition and social gathering. A number of competitions, divided into categories based on gender and age, feature Indians dressed in colorful costumes performing vigorous dances accompanied by rhythmic songs. The pow wow is set amid the natural beauty of the Sangre de Cristo Mountains and the Taos Valley, and it is held on the second weekend in July (Friday through Sunday). For more information visit www.taospueblopowwow.com.

Pow Wows are all about excitement and movement and color. To capture these qualities, use a zoom lens 200mm and longer, and be prepared to move around the dance arena following the action. If your lens or camera offers shake-reduction technology, make sure it is engaged to increase the chances of getting sharp images. However, also experiment with slower shutter speeds for more semi-abstract, artistic interpretations of the various dances. If you are shooting on a sunny day, use fill flash to help reduce contrast in your images, but remember you will have to get close to the action for the flash to be effective. Wide-angle lenses will be useful for storytelling shots featuring foreground subjects like the crowd, Indian drummers, and dancers waiting their turn to enter the arena.

If you wish to photograph dancers outside the arena—a good idea to get some semi-formal portraits of the participants—ask first.

Directions: From the Taos Plaza, drive north on US 64 for 2.4 miles. Turn right on D Ben Romero Road next to the Overland Sheepskin Company. Follow the road a short distance to the parking area.

North Central New Mexico Diversions: For a dose of history and culture, visit the museums on Museum Hill (www.museumhill.org), located a short drive from Santa Fe's plaza. The Museum of Spanish Colonial Art, the Museum of Indian Arts and Culture, the Museum of International Folk Art, and the Wheelwright Museum of the American Indian offer the visitor four distinct, world-class museums, all within walking distance. Milner Plaza, a large, open space featuring outdoor art and offering great views of Santa Fe and beyond, serves as the focal point of the museum zone. Have lunch at the Museum Hill Café, and don't forget to stop at the museum's gift shops, which offer a unique and eclectic mix of crafts, books, and gifts.

Rock formations, Tent Rocks National Monument

III. Central New Mexico

General Description: Central New Mexico is dominated by Albuquerque, the state's only metropolitan area. Founded by the Spanish in 1706, the original colonists chose a spot at the foot of the Sandia Mountains on the banks of the Rio Grande. Today, in addition to the impressive Sandias, this city of almost 800,000 features a Spanish colonial plaza, a segment of Historic Route 66, the world-class International Balloon Fiesta, and a national monument containing ancient petroglyphs.

Outside Albuquerque, this region includes a number of Spanish missions, a good ol' Wild West shooting festival, and a park protecting unique rock formations.

Tent Rocks National Monument (42)

Officially called the Kasha-Katuwe Tent Rocks National Monument (Kasha-Katuwe means "white cliffs" in the language of the nearby Cochiti Pueblo), this remarkable park features cone-shaped rock formations that are the product of volcanic eruptions that took place 6 million to 7 million years ago. The tent rocks vary in height from a few feet to 90 feet, and are decorated with various bands of gray, beige, and soft pink volcanic material. Access to the best views of the tent rocks is via a narrow canyon that has been carved over time by wind and water. Because of the orientation of the rocks within the canyon, I prefer photographing at Tent Rocks in the morning.

Of the two hiking trails in the park, I recommend the 1.5-mile (one way) moderate Canyon Trail, which follows the canyon floor before steeply climbing 630 feet to the top of a mesa. Use a wide-angle lens to capture the sinuous curves of the canyon as well as the grand vistas

---

Noted For: Historic Albuquerque, Sandia Mountains, Historic Route 66, International Balloon Fiesta, Bosque del Apache

Best Times: Late spring, early summer, fall, and during listed events

Exertion: Minimal to moderate

Peak Times: Spring: May; Summer: June; Fall: September and October; Winter: December; during listed events

Facilities: At developed sites

Parking: In lots, on the street and at trailheads

Sleeps and Eats: Albuquerque, Belen, Socorro

Sites and Events Included: Tent Rocks National Monument, Salinas Pueblo Missions National Monument, Old Town Albuquerque, San Felipe de Neri Church, Historic Route 66, Petroglyph National Monument, Albuquerque International Balloon Fiesta, End of Trail Wild West Jubilee, River of Lights

---

from the mesa's ridge. Include hikers in some of your pictures for a sense of scale.

Although the rocks are very graphic, they are somewhat bland in color, so consider using New Mexico's deep blue skies as a backdrop to your compositions. Bring your polarizer filter to saturate the blue sky and add contrast to your compositions.

Some of the best views of the tent rocks are from halfway up the trail's steep section. You will be higher than the rocks themselves and close enough to fill the frame (use a mid-telephoto zoom) with the unique formations. The ridge top also offers panoramic views of the surrounding landscape, including the Sandia, Sangre de Cristo, and Jemez Mountains, as well as the Rio Grande Valley.

Abó Mission ruins, Salinas Pueblo Missions National Monument

Directions: From Albuquerque, drive north on I-25 and take Exit 264. Turn right on NM 16 and drive about 8.5 miles to the "T" intersection (NM 22). Turn right on NM 22 and go another 2.8 miles, then turn left at the sign for the national monument. After another 1.8 miles, turn right at the marked sign for Tent Rocks. Less than a mile later the road will turn to dirt. Continue another 4.5 miles on this graded dirt road to the monument's parking area on the right.

Salinas Pueblo Missions National Monument

The Salinas Pueblo Missions National Monument was established to protect three separate missions—**Abó (43), Quarai (44), and Gran Quivira (45)**—located in a relatively remote area in Central New Mexico. In addition to the haunting ruins of the three missions, each of the sites features a variety of interesting structures such as kivas, cemeteries, and Indian dwellings. Each of the missions and surrounding structures is easily accessed via short, level trails.

If you wish to photograph all three missions in one outing, I suggest starting with the farthest one, Gran Quivira, then Quarai, and finally Abó. This order will not only leave you closer to Albuquerque at the end of your shoot, but also will allow you to take advantage of the morning light at Gran Quivira and Quarai, both of which photograph best early in the day. Abó will yield good images in either the morning or afternoon.

In general, Abó and Gran Quivira offer the most expansive vistas, while Quarai features the best preserved mission of the three. Each has ruins of Indian dwellings that will make great foreground subjects, and all offer quite a variety of angles and vantage points from which to photograph the churches. Abó and

Quarai are constructed of red brick, while Gran Quivira, unique in this respect, is made of grayish blue stone.

For each site you will need a wide-angle lens to take in the missions, structures, and surrounding landscapes, while a tripod will be useful to make sure you get tack-sharp images. A midrange zoom lens is also recommended to make tight compositions of the missions and for close-up, detail images of windows, portions of the dwellings, and so on. Put on your circular polarizer to saturate the blue sky and add contrast if needed.

Directions: Abó: From Albuquerque, drive south on I-25 for 35 miles. Take Exit 195 (for Belén) and follow the signs through town to NM 47. After about 18 miles, turn left (east) on US 60 and continue another 13 miles. Turn left at NM 513 and drive 0.5 mile to the mission.

Quarai: From the turnoff to Abó on US 60, travel east 9 miles to Mountainair. Turn left (north) on NM 55 and drive 8 miles to the Quarai sign. Turn left (west) and drive 1 mile to the mission.

Gran Quivira: From Mountainair, drive south on NM 55 for 25 miles to the ruins.

Albuquerque

Old Town (46)

Comprised of about ten blocks of historic adobe buildings containing shops, restaurants, and galleries, Albuquerque's Old Town is the city's historic center. A tree-shaded oasis in the middle of a modern metropolis, its plaza features a picturesque gazebo that serves as the stage for many local events. With its *portales* (porches), wooden benches, *vigas,* and other

Church at Quarai, Salinas Pueblo Missions National Monument

San Felipe de Neri Church, Old Town, Albuquerque

features of Spanish Pueblo architecture, much of the Old Town retains the look of yesteryear, when the Camino Real de Tierra Adentro (Inland Royal Way) went right through it.

Albuquerque's Old Town is a fun place to explore and photograph. Its maze of cobbled walkways, courtyards, and alleys lead to hidden patios, gardens, and religious shrines. Wide-angle and midrange lenses will be most useful in Old Town, together with a tripod for photographing architecture. Subjects around the plaza include its gazebo, architectural details, people, and Indian vendors under *portales.*

Beyond the plaza, explore the alleys and courtyards looking for interesting doors, chile *ristras,* religious shrines, and other photogenic subjects. Afternoons and early evenings are good times to photograph Old Town, since you'll be able to capture Old Town's vibrancy in your people pictures.

Directions: From the intersection of I-25 and I-40 in Albuquerque, drive west on I-40 to Exit 157A (Rio Grande Boulevard) and turn left (south). Old Town is located northeast of Rio Grande Boulevard and Central Avenue.

San Felipe de Neri Church (47)
Built in 1793 after the original mission was destroyed by floods, San Felipe de Neri Church is located on Old Town Plaza's north side. Featuring twin bell towers, a front courtyard, and traditional adobe Spanish colonial architecture, the church is listed on the National Register of Historic Places. Its interior includes lovely stained windows, wood paneling, a stamped metal ceiling, and an elaborate altar.

San Felipe de Neri faces south, so the ideal time of the year to photograph its façade in sunlight is during winter. Because of lighter foot and motorized traffic, mornings are best to capture the church without those distracting

elements. A wide-angle lens will allow you to take overall pictures of the structure, but be careful with immovable distractions like power poles and trees. Looking-up shots can also be effective, but be aware that wide-angle shots from below can look distorted, requiring post-trip manipulation in your computer. If you are visiting during Christmas, don't miss photographing the mission at twilight when it is surrounded by *farolitos.*

Inside the church, photo subjects include the beautiful stained glass windows (bring a midrange zoom to take frame-filling compositions) as well as the altar. Try to visit when the crowds are thin to avoid unwanted distractions, but also consider including people in your shots to add a human touch.

Directions: See directions for Old Town.

Historic Route 66 (48)
Credited with jump-starting Albuquerque's explosive growth beginning in the 1940s, Route 66 becomes Central Avenue within the city. This urban stretch of road is lined with neon signs, motor courts, diners, trading posts, gas stations, and other establishments from the heyday of the Mother Road. Some of these sights are still operational, while others have seen better days.

Although there are photo-worthy subjects all along Albuquerque's portion of Route 66, one of my favorite areas is Nob Hill, one of the city's hippest addresses and located adjacent to the University of New Mexico (around Central and Carlisle). Marked on either end by neon arches, the mile-long stretch of road is home to the Nob Hill Shopping Center (an eclectic mix of architectural and design styles, such as Territorial revival, Art Moderne, and Art Deco), abundant neon signs, and the historic Jones Motor Company, a car dealership/gas station business that now houses a fashionable restaurant.

Another good location for Route 66 photography is downtown Albuquerque, where you will find a number of very photogenic neon signs, a vibrant night life, and historic theaters such as the Pueblo Deco style KiMo Theater.

Above all, Albuquerque's stretch of Historic Route 66 is about energy, vibrancy, movement, and color. Therefore, the best time to photograph Route 66 is during early evening twilight, when the streets are abustle and neon signs look fantastic against the deep blue skies. To add movement to your pictures, include moving-traffic light streaks in your compositions by using long (multi-second) shutter speeds. A tripod is essential for this type of photography. For a more melancholic interpretation of Route 66, also consider photographing in daylight the many dilapidated signs along the road. Turning these into black and white or sepia tone images would make for a nice addition to your New Mexico image collection.

Directions: To reach Nob Hill, take the I-25 exit for Central Avenue. Turn right (east) on Central and drive 1.5 miles to the neon arch on Central and Girard. Nob Hill stretches another mile from here to a second neon arch at Central and Washington. Park near Central and Carlisle and you'll be in the middle of the action. To reach downtown Albuquerque, take the I-25 exit for Central Avenue. Turn right (west) on Central and park around Central and Sixth for a good location.

Petroglyph National Monument (49)

West Mesa, a 17-mile long table of land west of the Rio Grande, was formed about 150,000

Streaking car lights and storefronts on Route 66/Central Avenue, Nob Hill, Albuquerque

Petroglyphs, Rinconada Canyon, Petroglyph National Monument, Albuquerque

years ago as a result of volcanic eruptions. Over time, the eastern edge of the new land formation eroded into a rocky escarpment made up of large basalt boulders broken away from the lava rock. Eventually humans arrived on the scene and began pecking a variety of animal, human, and geometric forms on the rocks by exposing the lighter gray beneath the dark desert varnish. Archaeologists believe most of these figures, or petroglyphs, are 400 to 700 years old, with some believed to be as old as 3,000 years. Petroglyph National Monument was established to protect the more than 20,000 images within the park.

The monument features three canyons where you can photograph petroglyphs: Rinconada, Boca Negra, and Piedras Marcadas.

My favorite canyons are Rinconada and Boca Negra, since they are easily accessible and contain hundreds of petroglyphs. Remember that you will be photographing in an urban area, so be prepared to use your creative abilities to avoid unwanted distractions such as power lines and poles.

The Rinconada Canyon petroglyphs can be reached via a sandy, 1.2-mile (one way) trail that travels west to the end of the volcanic escarpment. As you get farther from the trailhead you will soon see petroglyphs on the south-facing and east-facing slopes of the shallow canyon. Continue on the trail until you see some petroglyphs that you would like to photograph. Some of the best petroglyphs are near the end of the trail.

For most close-up shots of the petroglyphs you will need to do some easy rock climbing. Be careful with sharp edges and the uneven terrain. Mornings are best for images of the rocks at first light, but late afternoons work well for low-contrast photos in the shade. Use a wide-angle lens for broad images showing the petroglyphs in the foreground and the canyon in the distance. For tighter compositions use a mid-range zoom.

Boca Negra Canyon is more developed than Rinconada and offers three easy, partly paved trails with interpretive signs. The longest trail will take about 30–45 minutes to hike, so the physical exertion will be minimal. In my opinion Boca Negra contains some of the best petroglyphs in the monument, although Rinconada offers a more solitary experience.

Directions: To reach the Rinconada Canyon trailhead, drive north on Unser from I-40 to St. Joseph Avenue. The parking area will be on your left (west). The monument's visitor center is located 1 mile north of Rinconada Canyon on your left (west). The Boca Negra Canyon parking area is located 2 miles north of the visitor center (still on Unser) on the right (east).

Albuquerque International Balloon Fiesta (50)

Held for nine consecutive days beginning the first week of October, the Albuquerque International Balloon Fiesta is the largest ballooning

Hot air balloons on ground and aloft, Albuquerque Balloon Fiesta

event in the world. Hosting over 700 balloons participating in a variety of events such as mass ascensions, dawn patrols, balloon glows, and special shapes rodeos, the festival is a colorful and exciting event to photograph. The balloon events are held in Balloon Fiesta Park, a dedicated 365-acre field complete with a carnival-style midway featuring food stands, crafts vendors, entertainment, and other amenities. For a complete schedule of events, and to purchase advance tickets, visit www.balloonfiesta.com.

Arrive early when photographing the mass ascensions; this will give you time to scout the area and select a good vantage point. As it gets lighter, be ready for fast and furious handheld photography as large groups of balloons are sent in droves to the sky. Concentrate first on images of balloon teams getting ready to launch, the "zebras" (referees) directing traffic, and propane blasts creating colorful flames under the balloons. As the balloons take flight, compose vertical and horizontal images of different groups of balloons and single balloons from every angle you can think of. Later you will be able to sit down and edit your take.

During the spectacular balloon glows, hundreds of balloons fire their burners in unison and light up the night sky. Get close to the balloons as regular blasts of propane illuminate the colorful globes in the dark. Step (way) back to take overall pictures of large groups of balloons. Make sure you use a high ISO (at least 800) and wide apertures (f4.0 or so) since light will be low and the action fast. Try not to include too much black sky as it will look grainy because of the high ISO. Use a wide-angle lens to photograph the balloons, the people around them, and overall shots. A zoom in the 70mm–200mm range will come in handy for close-up shots of the action.

Other photo-worthy events are the special shapes rodeo (extra popular with kids), featuring balloons shaped like dragons, stagecoaches, animals, and other objects; and the dawn patrols, when about a dozen balloons take to the skies in darkness.

Directions: Get off on I-25 Exit 134 (Tramway) and follow the signs to the parking lot at Balloon Fiesta Park.

End of Trail Wild West Jubilee (51)

Held over four days in June at Founders Ranch east of Albuquerque, the End of Trail Wild West Jubilee is the largest shooting competition and Wild West festival in the country. Each year over a thousand authentically dressed participants portraying cowboys, soldiers, gunfighters, and other Western characters converge in a 100-acre, living-history encampment to compete in a variety of shooting events. In addition to the shooting competitions, the jubilee features Western-themed shops, food, shooting demonstrations, live entertainment, and even stagecoach rides.

To take advantage of the Wild West Jubilee's many photo opportunities, plan on spending the better part of a day at the festival. Log on to www.sass.net for a complete schedule of events and to plan your shoot. My personal favorite event is the mounted shooting competition, where cowboys and cowgirls shoot at red balloons while negotiating a cone-marked course on their horses. Bring your long zoom lens to photograph these events since in most cases you will be shooting from a distance. Afterwards do not be afraid to approach some of the participants and ask to take their pictures. These folks are some of the friendliest I have ever encountered and are more than happy to pose for a few pictures. Also ask them for their "shooting alias," as participants are required to take on the personas of Old West characters and will happily share their "pasts" with you.

I also like to wander around the encampment and photograph the activity there. You

Cowboy on horse, mounted shooting competition, End of Trail Wild West Jubilee, Edgewood

will encounter all sorts of photo ops like more Western characters, details of Western goods such as saddles and rifles, a cooking fire surrounded by pots and pans, and even a photographer's shop. For these shots use your wide-angle and midrange zooms, since you will be able to get close to your subjects. In addition, some of the entertainment events, especially the staged gunfights and gun demonstrations, are fun to photograph. And don't forget an establishing shot of the busy encampment to complete your photo collection.

Directions: From Albuquerque, take I-40 east and drive 20 miles to Exit 181 (Sedillo Hill Road). Drive east on Sedillo/US 66 to NM 217. Turn right (south) and drive 5 miles to Juan Tomas Road. Turn left (east) and drive 1.5 miles to Barton Road. Turn left (north) and drive 0.75 mile to the entrance of Founders Ranch.

River of Lights (52)

Started in 1997, the Albuquerque River of Lights has quickly become one of the city's most popular Christmas holiday events. The walk-through show is held in the Rio Grande Botanic Garden and features hundreds of dazzling, twinkling-light displays in the shape of animals, fish, flowers, buildings, and other objects. Local choirs provide a musical backdrop to the event, and hot drinks and food are available. It will be cold, so dress accordingly.

Because of low-light conditions and consequently long shutter speeds, bring a tripod to photograph the many whimsical light sculptures you will encounter at River of Lights. Consider including people in your compositions—they will probably be blurred—to add movement and excitement to your images. Because many of the displays change color periodically, take a variety of pictures of the same subject.

To add variety to your shots, consider zooming in (or out) during your multi-second exposures. This will make your subjects appear as if they were exploding, adding life to the already colorful subjects. Try this technique different times using different shutter speeds, as the effects will vary considerably from shot to shot. In general, I prefer shots where the subject, although exploding, is still recognizable.

Directions: From the intersection of I-40 and I-25 in Albuquerque, drive west on I-40 to the Rio Grande Boulevard exit (157A). Turn left (south) on Rio Grande Boulevard. Turn right (west) on Central Avenue. Turn right (northwest) on New York Avenue. The parking lot for the Rio Grande Botanic Garden will be on your left.

Central New Mexico Diversions: Take the Sandia Peak Tramway (www.sandiapeak.com), the longest aerial tramway in the world, to the top of Sandia Peak at 10,378 feet. Make dinner reservations at the High Finance Restaurant atop the peak, and enjoy the spectacular views of Albuquerque's city lights.

Truck decorated with Christmas lights, River of Lights, Albuquerque BioPark

Capulin Volcano National Monument, near Raton

IV. Northeast New Mexico

SEASONAL RATINGS: SPRING ★ ★ ★ ★ SUMMER ★ ★ ★ FALL ★ ★ ★ ★ WINTER ★

General Description: Home to vast grasslands, volcanic remnants, and the state's portion of the Santa Fe Trail, Northeast New Mexico is where the western end of the Great Plains meets the eastern slopes of the Rocky Mountains. It was through the state's northeast corridor—first with the establishment of the Santa Fe Trail and later with the arrival of the railroad—that New Mexico became prosperous, acting as an important cultural and economic link between the east and the west. Today, some of the region's communities, such as Las Vegas and Raton, still retain the feel of the Old West.

Fort Union National Monument (53)

Established in 1851 to guard the Santa Fe Trail, Fort Union eventually became the largest fort in the Southwest. Functioning as both a military garrison and territorial arsenal for the region, the fort became an important stop along the famous trail. Although mostly in ruins today, Fort Union features a number of partially standing, photogenic ruins that once served as officers' quarters, a military prison, a mechanics' corral, and other structures. A number of discarded wagon wheels, cannon, and a Civil War wagon replica are strewn about the grounds and add to the frontier ambiance.

Because Fort Union stands on a barren plain far from mountains or other obstructions, it photographs well in either the morning or the afternoon. However, the oft-photographed mechanics corral, featuring wagon wheels and ruined wagons, faces west, so it photographs best in the afternoon. In addition to the mechanics corral, some of my favorite subjects include the hospital, the military prison, and the long row of officers' quarters.

Noted For: Santa Fe Trail, Fort Union National Monument, Civil War past, historic buildings, expansive grasslands

Best Times: Late spring, early summer, fall, and during listed events

Exertion: Minimal to moderate

Peak Times: Spring: May; summer: June; fall: September and October; winter: December; during listed events

Facilities: At developed sites

Parking: In lots, on the street, and at trailheads

Sleeps and Eats: Las Vegas, Raton

Sites and Events Included: Fort Union National Monument, Fort Union Civil War Reenactment, Capulin Volcano National Monument

Photographing the fort's structures is easy via a flat, 1.6-mile loop trail that starts and finishes at the visitor center. Use a wide-angle lens to take overall shots, placing a strong element such as a cannon in the foreground to tell a story and bring your viewers into the picture. Lenses 100mm or longer will be useful when photographing architectural details like a window, repeating chimney ruins, and so on. As with most architectural subjects, use a tripod for tack-sharp images. And if the skies are at least partially sunny, screw a polarizer onto your lenses to add saturation to the sky.

Directions: Fort Union is located 20 miles north of Las Vegas, NM. Drive north on I-25 to Exit 366 (NM 161). Turn left (west) and drive 8 miles to the monument.

Fort Union Civil War Reenactment (54)

Shortly after the start of the Civil War in 1861, the Confederate army began moving into New Mexico to take control of the Santa Fe Trail. In

March of 1862, during the Battle of Glorieta Pass (about 20 miles southeast of Santa Fe), the Confederate invasion was halted and turned back by a force made up of Colorado and New Mexico volunteers and U.S. regulars from Fort Union. The Confederates' subsequent retreat to Texas effectively ended Civil War activity in the Southwest.

Every July, Fort Union hosts a Civil War re-enactment (called "Living History Programs"), complete with military drills, gun firing demonstrations, military bands, and an encampment. Get there early to photograph the encampment's tents, the soldiers preparing breakfast over open pit fires, and the ceremonial raising of the flag. Attend the military band concert and get up-close shots of the different musicians and their Civil War–era instruments. Both wide-angle and midrange lenses will work here.

When photographing close to firing guns, wear earplugs to protect yourself. Lenses 100mm or longer will allow you to get tight shots of soldiers firing their guns and cannon. Don't forget to photograph storytelling Civil War details such as portions of soldiers' clothing, cannon wheels, firearms, tents, and so on.

Directions: See directions to Fort Union National Monument, above.

Capulin Volcano National Monument (55)

Capulin Volcano National Monument was established to protect a volcanic cinder cone formed about 50,000–60,000 years ago—just yesterday by geologic standards. Part grassland and part forest, the volcano's vegetation consists of a variety of pine trees and shrubs such as ponderosa pine, juniper, mountain mahogany, and scrub oak. A 2-mile paved road

Wagon wheels, mechanics' corral, Fort Union National Monument

Civil War reenactors fire a cannon at Fort Union National Monument (sepia-toned)

and two short trails provide easy access to the volcano's rim, which rises over 8,000 feet above the surrounding terrain. The top of the volcano offers panoramic views of the surrounding terrain, including far-away extinct volcanoes and mesas.

Bring the widest lens you have to photograph Capulin Volcano's gaping maw from the easy 1-mile Crater Rim Trail loop. As an alternative, consider making a panoramic composition by taking a number of shots and stitching them together in the computer. Because the cinder block volcano is dark, include clouds in your composition if possible to add interest and texture. Although the views of the mesas and other volcanoes from atop Capulin are grand, they are too far off to photograph effectively.

In addition to up-close shots, make sure you photograph Capulin Volcano from a distance to show its conical top. These images can be taken only from outside the monument. One suggestion is to drive north on NM 325, past the park's entrance, and pull over on the side of the road once you have cleared the volcano's north

side. From here you can hike around the monument's surrounding terrain, which includes a variety of objects such as volcanic rocks, small trees, and shrubs, which you can include in the foreground of your compositions. A number of dirt roads near the monument also offer good vantage points for overall images of the volcano.

Directions: From Raton, drive 30 miles east on US 64/87 to the village of Capulin. Turn left (north) on NM 325 and drive 3 miles to the monument's entrance on your left (east).

Northeast New Mexico Diversions: For a unique lodging experience, spend a night at the historic Plaza Hotel in Las Vegas (www.plazahotel-nm.com). Originally built in 1882, the Plaza features Victorian elegance combined with all the modern amenities. While in town, spend some time admiring the more than 900 buildings listed on the National Register of Historic Places. The Las Vegas Citizens' Committee for Historic Preservation offers guided and self-guided historic tours (www.lasvegas nmcchp.com).

Ruins, Gila Cliff Dwellings National Monument

V. Southwest New Mexico

General Description: Characterized by abundant sunshine and dry weather perfect for growing chile, Southwest New Mexico features expansive landscapes punctuated by relatively small mountain ranges. Throughout the region a number of long-abandoned ghost towns still stand as reminders of the area's mining days, even as the Very Large Array's radio telescopes scan the skies searching for extraterrestrial life.

Just south of Socorro along the Rio Grande, the region's most spectacular natural display takes place every winter when thousands of migratory birds make their yearly pilgrimage to Bosque del Apache. Southwest New Mexico also offers some of the most authentic Mexican festivals in the state. The Gila Cliff Dwellings, within the Gila National Forest near Silver City, offer a glimpse into the area's prehistoric past.

Bosque del Apache National Wildlife Refuge (56)

Managed by the U.S. Fish and Wildlife Service, Bosque del Apache ("Forest of the Apache" in Spanish) is undoubtedly one of the premier bird photography destinations in the country. The heart of the refuge consists of almost 13,000 acres of moist bottomlands that become the winter home to tens of thousands of sandhill cranes, snow geese, and many other migratory birds. The rest of the Bosque is made up of arid foothills and mesas, which rise to the Chupadera Mountains on the west and the San Pascual Mountains on the east, providing beautiful backdrops for the daily spectacles put on by the birds.

The best time to photograph birds in Bosque is between early November and mid-February, when the bulk of the migratory birds

---

Noted For: Bosque del Apache National Wildlife Refuge, the Very Large Array, mining ghost towns, the Gila Wilderness, Organ Mountains, Old Mesilla, authentic Mexican celebrations, chile

Best Times: Late spring, early summer, fall, and during listed events

Exertion: Minimal to moderate

Peak Times: Spring: May; summer: June; fall: September and October; winter: December; during listed events

Facilities: At developed sites

Parking: In lots, on the street, and at trailheads

Sleeps and Eats: Socorro, Silver City, Las Cruces, Truth or Consequences; limited facilities at Lordsburg, Deming, and Magdalena

Sites and Events Included: Bosque del Apache National Wildlife Refuge, Very Large Array, Shakespeare Ghost Town, Steins Ghost Town, Silver City Historic District, City of Rocks State Park, Gila National Forest, Gila Cliff Dwellings National Monument, Pinos Altos Ghost Town, Organ Mountains, Old Mesilla Plaza, San Albino Church, Cinco de Mayo Celebration, Mexican Independence Day Celebration

---

visit the refuge. Mornings feature the famous "fly-out," when, just as the sun is about to clear the nearby hills, flocks of birds take flight in unison, filling the sky with their winged shapes as they head north to their feeding grounds. The most popular area to photograph the fly-out is the flight deck observation area. Afternoon fly-ins are also fun to photograph, although in my opinion they are not as spectacular. During the day, you can spend time hiking the short trails,

Snow geese in flight, Bosque del Apache National Wildlife Refuge

driving the auto tour loop, and photographing the birds feeding.

When photographing birds, look for simple, uncluttered backgrounds such as distant hills and areas of sky with pleasing clouds and colors. Bring the longest lenses in your arsenal for frame-filling compositions, but don't forget to use wide-angle and normal zooms for landscape shots of the area.

Because you will be photographing in winter during the coldest times of the day, make sure you dress accordingly, and that you bring extra batteries (kept warm inside your jacket) and memory cards to capture the fast-moving action.

Directions: From Socorro (which is about an hour south of Albuquerque on I-25), drive south on I-25 for 9 miles to Exit 139. Drive west on US 380 for 0.25 mile, then turn right on NM 1 and drive another 9 miles to the Bosque's visitor center.

National Radio Astronomy Observatory Very Large Array (57)

Located just west of Magdalena on the vast, featureless San Agustin Plains, the National Radio Astronomy Observatory Very Large Array (VLA) is one of the world's most important astronomical radio observatories. The VLA consists of 27 radio antennas (dishes) deployed in a Y-shaped grid; each arm is 13 miles long. The dishes, 80 feet in diameter, are moved about every four months, with some configurations bringing them close together while others space them farther apart. For a schedule of dates and configurations, visit www.nrao.edu.

Because the VLA is on a wide open plain, both morning and afternoon photography will yield good results. I suggest you check the VLA website before your visit to make sure the antennas are arrayed in a tight configuration. Otherwise you will be limited to photographing solitary dishes here and there.

Start your visit by taking the short walk from the visitor center to the antenna located at the end of an interpretive trail. This will give you the opportunity to get very close to one of the dishes and appreciate their size (they look tiny from a distance). If the dishes are in a tight configuration, use a wide-angle lens to photograph the main dish in the foreground with others in the distance. The dishes actually pivot in place from time to time, so if you don't like their particular orientation, wait a few minutes and they will move. Include people in some of your compositions for scale. Consider using a lens 100mm or longer for tight compositions of one, two, or more groups of antennas.

Directions: The VLA is located 20 miles west of Magdalena and 50 miles west of Socorro on US 60. From US 60, turn south on NM 52, then west on the VLA access road, which is well marked. Signs will point you to the visitor center.

Shakespeare Ghost Town (58)

Declared a National Historic Site in 1970, Shakespeare Ghost Town is New Mexico's best example of a true late-1800s pioneer town. Notorious outlaws such as Billy the Kid, Curly Bill Brocius, and the Clantons are said to have visited Shakespeare.

Privately owned but open to the public one weekend per month, Shakespeare (formerly known as Mexican Springs and Grant) features a large number of well-preserved structures flanking its main street, including a saloon, a hotel, a mail station, a blacksmith shop, and an assay office (where precious metals were tested

Radio telescopes, Very Large Array, near Magdalena

for purity). The interiors of eight of these buildings can be visited during the scheduled tours, providing a glimpse into the daily lives of the town's former inhabitants. Throughout the year, Shakespeare also plays host to special living history events featuring gunfights, a blacksmith, and reenactors dressed in period costumes. For a schedule of tours and events, visit www.shakespeareghostown.com.

Although visiting Shakespeare is possible only by participating in a tour (either privately by prior arrangement or during a scheduled tour), the pace is slow enough to allow for effective photography. Bring a tripod and a wide-angle lens for interior shots, as you will be working in tight, low-light conditions.

During the tour, concentrate on details like bullet-riddled walls behind the saloon's bar, dilapidated chairs lined up against a wall, and blacksmith tools hanging from the rafters. Also, take a number of overall shots of each room to place interesting details in context. Outside, work on images showing the surrounding terrain to create a sense of place in this otherwise desolate area, but also photo-

Stagecoach and log cabin, Steins Ghost Town, near Lordsburg

graph individual buildings' façades, windows, and doors to round out your collection. Back home, consider converting some of your images to black and white, perhaps with some added grain for a historic, Old West feel.

Directions: Shakespeare is 2.5 miles south of Lordsburg. From I-10, take Exit 2 (Lordsburg's Main Street) and turn south. Follow the signs to Shakespeare.

Steins Ghost Town (59)

First established as a station on the Southern Pacific Railroad line in the 1880s, Steins is one of New Mexico's best-preserved ghost towns. Named after U.S. Army officer Enoch Stein, the town's population reached about 1,300 during its heyday in the early 1900s, despite continuous attacks by Indians and outlaws. In 1944 the Southern Pacific shut down operations at the station and the town was abandoned. Today, the privately owned town features a general store, living quarters, barns, a stagecoach, and other structures. Visitors are welcome to explore the grounds for free, and the owners offer a guided tour of some of the buildings' interiors for a small fee.

Start your visit outside, photographing the tongue-in-cheek cemetery (a tombstone reads "I told ya I wuz sik"), the general store, overall shots of the town showing its desert landscape, and my personal favorite, the stagecoach.

Make sure you have enough time to take the guided tour when you visit. More than any other ghost town in the state, Steins offers the opportunity to photograph everyday objects such as books, children's clothing, kitchen crockery, colorful bottles, and so on. Note that some of these rooms are recreations of the original.

Directions: Steins is located 19 miles west of Lordsburg off I-10's Exit 3. The ghost town is immediately north of the exit.

Warren House, Silver City

Silver City

Historic District (60)

Established in 1870 after silver was discovered in the nearby hills, Silver City soon became the object of Indian raids led by Cochise, Geronimo, and others, and attracted the attention of outlaws like Billy the Kid, Butch Cassidy, and the Wild Bunch. Despite its rocky start, the town rapidly expanded and soon became one of the most important trading and "entertainment" center in the region. Elegant Victorian mansions, saloons, hotels, and restaurants sprouted along and the city's center, or "Silver" as it's called by the locals, quickly transformed itself from a tent camp to a booming city. Even after the bottom dropped out of the silver market in 1893, Silver City quickly recovered and has become a cultural, tourist, and outdoor recreation center.

Many of the buildings around Bullard and Broadway, the town's center and part of its historic district, date to the late 1800s and early 1900s. From the intersection look north on Bullard and take overall images of the historic buildings as they recede from you. If a lot of traffic is present, consider using long (multi-second) shutter speeds to blur the moving vehicles and add a touch of action to your compositions. These shots are particularly effective at night. Also explore the few blocks west of the intersection on Broadway, where

Standing rocks (hardened volcanic tuff) and grasses, City of Rocks State Park, near Silver City

you will find the Silver City Museum, housed in an 1881 Victorian mansion formerly owned by early pioneer H. B. Ailman; and the historic Palace Hotel, both of which face south.

Continuing west on Broadway, at its intersection with Cooper you will find the imposing, east-facing Grant County Courthouse, built in 1930 and featuring brick construction with Art Deco details. Other photo-worthy subjects in Silver City's historic district include the Warren House on Market Street, a beautiful 1881 Italianate red brick structure; the salmon-colored, circa 1908 St. Vincent de Paul Church (Market and Bayard), featuring Missionrevival construction and two towers; the 1934 Pueblo Deco El Sol Theater (404 N. Bullard); and the colorful Yankie Street, the town's artists' quarters.

For a bird's eye view of the city, follow Arizona Street south and walk up the short hill to La Capilla Park. The park offers grand views of Silver City below, which looks especially appealing at twilight when the city lights are on.

Directions: From US 180 (north side of town), turn south on NM 90 (Hudson Street), then right on Broadway to Bullard. Coming north on NM 90, turn left on Broadway to Bullard. Street parking is available near the intersection of Broadway and Bullard.

City of Rocks State Park (61)
Relatively small at 680 acres, City of Rocks State Park nevertheless contains a fascinating group of volcanic ash monoliths that are found in only a handful of other places in the world. The rocks were formed about 30 million years

ago as the welded ash was sculpted by wind and water over time. When seen from a distance, the standing rocks look like a collection of houses, chimneys, and other buildings towering above the surrounding plain, thus giving the park its name. A couple of short trails provide easy access to photograph the rock formations.

Because City of Rocks is exposed in all directions, either early or late photography will yield excellent results. I recommend spending at least one night car-camping in the park (fee required) to photograph during the best light possible (the park's gates are closed at night-time). If photographing under cloudless skies, watch for high contrast between the sunny and shaded sides of the rocks. Use the contrast to your advantage and create semi-abstract, chiaroscuro (light and dark) images of the rocks.

To take overall pictures of the park's skyline, hike the easy 3.25-mile Hydra Walking Trail, which circles the entire park. For up-close compositions of the rocks, follow the short, interior trail that bisects the park. Add interest and context to your pictures by using a wide-angle lens to include indigenous plants such as yucca or cacti in the foreground of your compositions. For intimate images of native vegetation, spend some time photographing at the park's desert botanical garden.

Directions: From Silver City, drive south on US 180 for 32 miles, then northeast 4 miles on NM 61 to the park's entrance. From Deming, drive north on US 180 for 24 miles, then northeast 4 miles to the park's entrance.

Gila National Forest (62)

Administered by the USDA Forest Service, the Gila National Forest is one of the most remote and least developed forests in the Southwest. Encompassing about 3.3 million acres, the forest includes the Gila Wilderness, established in 1924 as the country's first to be designated as

such. Known for its rugged beauty, the area offers relatively easy access to great photographic opportunities despite its difficult terrain.

For panoramic views of the Black Range and the Rio Grande Valley, drive to Emory Pass Vista off NM 152 a few miles west of Kingston. From here the views to the east are spectacular. Use a wide-angle lens to include some of the trees below you in the foreground, as a number of mountain ridges fade in the distance. Be there at first light for best results.

If you prefer hiking for your shots, try one of the trails that begin at the parking lot for the Gila Cliff Dwellings north of Silver City. From here you can access the west fork of the Gila River, featuring forested canyons, many river crossings, ancient cliff dwellings, and even hot springs. Bring your wide-angle lens to photograph the variety of landscapes you will encounter here, and be prepared to get your feet wet!

For a comprehensive list of trails and other information about the Gila National Forest, visit www2.srs.fs.fed.us/r3/gila/.

Directions: Emory Pass Vista is located on NM 152 approximately 30 miles west of I-25's Exit 63. To reach the parking lot for the Gila Cliff Dwellings from Silver City, drive 42 miles north on NM 15. Turn left at the sign for Gila Cliff Dwellings National Monument and drive one mile to the parking lot.

Gila Cliff Dwellings National Monument (63)

Located within the Gila Wilderness Area, the Gila Cliff Dwellings National Monument offers a glimpse into the homes and lives of the Mogollon people, who lived in the area from the late 13th century through the14th. The dwellings themselves, consisting of about 40 rooms in 5 natural caves, date from the late 1200s. Nestled 180 feet above a narrow canyon, the southeast-facing dwellings can be reached via an unpaved 1-mile loop. Though short, the trail is steep and rocky in places.

The first portion of the trail follows a small creek along the forested bottom of the canyon. Your first glimpse of the cliff dwellings will come as you begin the steep section of the trail. You will need a lens 150mm or longer to take a frame-filling picture from here. After you clear the forest, look for compositions that include the dwellings in the distance as well as the surrounding canyon. Once you reach the ruins, a wide-angle lens and a midrange zoom will be useful in photographing the stone dwellings and surrounding landscape, as well as architectural details.

When photographing during cloudless days, the high contrast between the dark dwellings and the bright canyon will pose a challenge. Consider taking pictures of dwellings that are completely in the shade to avoid contrast problems.

Directions: From Silver City, drive 42 miles north on NM 15. Turn left at the sign for Gila Cliff Dwellings National Monument and drive 1 mile to the trailhead's parking lot.

Pinos Altos Ghost Town (64)

Established in 1860 after a prospector found a handful of gold nuggets in a nearby creek, Pinos Altos population reached 9,000 during

Black Range Mountains in late fall from Emory Pass, Gila National Forest

Opera House, Pinos Altos Ghost Town, Pinos Altos

the 1880s and 90s. In the early 1900s, as the area's minerals petered out, so did the town. Today, the town's Main Street looks like a movie set for a Western, complete with a saloon, a fort replica, and an opera house. Many of the remaining buildings date to the 1800s and have been partially restored and decorated with original period artifacts.

One of the town's most photogenic buildings is the Pinos Altos Opera House, a brick and wood structure featuring two columns flanking its door. The opera house faces west so it photographs best in late afternoon. A wide-angle lens will be useful when photographing this and other structures in Pinos Altos.

A few doors down from the opera house is the Buckhorn Saloon, a former watering hole (circa 1860s) and now a popular restaurant. The saloon's weathered exterior features wooden *vigas*, hitching bars, and a portal. The Buckhorn photographs best in the afternoon. Other photo-worthy buildings in Pinos Altos include the Hearst Methodist Church (circa 1898), now home to a museum and art gallery; a log cabin from the 1860s and now housing the Pinos Altos Historical Museum; and the Pinos Altos Volunteer Fire and Rescue House, notable for its wood construction and red trim (although the firehouse is not a historic building, it was constructed to fit within the town's late 1800s architecture). These last three buildings face east and photograph best in the morning.

Directions: From Silver City, drive 6 miles north on NM 15.

Desert vegetation and Organ Mountains, near Las Cruces

Las Cruces

Organ Mountains (65)

Named after the craggy, needle-like granite outcrops that resemble organ pipes, the Organ Mountains are located east of Las Cruces and provide the scenic backdrop to many of this city's photographs. Together with the Franklin Mountains to the south, the Organ Mountains are part of a 54,000-acre nature preserve managed by the Bureau of Land Management. Although rugged and arid, the north/south range is easily accessible from developed areas on both its east and west flanks.

The Organ Mountains' best access point for morning photography is Aguirre Spring Road, a paved, 3-mile track that meanders its way to the Aguirre Spring Campground. For first-light photography, park your car just outside the gate (it opens at 8 AM), then walk along the road looking for pleasing compositions. This side of the mountains features large granite boulders and a variety of large cacti that can be used as foreground subjects. The possibilities are endless, so scout around until you find a composition you like. In the spring you will also find colorful wildflowers in the area, but be aware that springtime in New Mexico can be very windy. Use a wide-angle lens to photograph this grand landscape, and a tripod to get tack-sharp images.

The mountain's west side can be accessed via Baylor Canyon Road, a graded dirt track running close to the base of the mountains. Though lacking the large boulders found on the east side of the mountains, the panoramic views of the Organs are spectacular from this side. From the southern end of Baylor Canyon Road (or thereabouts), consider taking a number of shots and stitching them as a panorama later. For up-close views of the mountains, park at the La Cueva Picnic Area and hike the easy 1.5 miles to the ruins of the old resort at Dripping Springs.

Directions: The Organ Mountains are located about 11 miles east of Las Cruces. To reach the mountain's east side, from I-25's Exit 6, take US 70 east, drive over San Agustin Pass, and turn right on Aguirre Spring Road. To reach the west side, from I-25's Exit 1, take University Boulevard east until it turns into Baylor Canyon Road.

Old Mesilla Plaza (66)

Founded around 1848 when the region was still part of Mexico, Old Mesilla (also known as La Mesilla or simply Mesilla)—located a few minutes south of Las Cruces—soon became an important trading center between San Antonio and San Diego. In 1853, in the Gadsden Purchase, Old Mesilla became a part of the United States. The treaty was consummated by the raising of the U.S. flag on the plaza. Today, the village's picturesque center features a number of historic buildings, a gazebo, and the San Albino Church (circa 1900).

As usual when photographing architecture, look for compositions that show the historic buildings at an angle to add depth to your pictures, although straight-on images work well with symmetrical buildings. Include the plaza and the surrounding buildings in one image to show context, and don't forget the always-important architectural details to round out your collection. Buildings around the plaza that are of particular historical interest include the Old Courthouse, where in 1881 Billy the Kid was tried for murder and sentenced to hang (he later escaped), and the oldest documented brick building in New Mexico (ca. 1860). The Old Courthouse is located on the southeast corner of the plaza, while the brick house is on the southwest corner. Both currently house gift shops.

Facing south and located on the plaza's north side is **San Albino Church (67)**, one of New Mexico's most striking churches. The all-brick building features twin bell towers topped by white crosses and a statue of the Virgin Mary up front. The immaculate interior has a beautiful vaulted ceiling framed in lustrous wood, while the brick walls are decorated with religious icons. You will need a wide-angle lens to take overall images of the church, inside or out. A lens 50mm or longer will be useful when photographing details such as the religious icons. Consider taking pictures that include the plaza and its gazebo in the foreground and the church behind. Be careful to avoid distracting elements such as cars parked in the small lot in front of the church.

Directions: From the intersection of I-25's Exit 1/University Avenue to the Old Mesilla Plaza it is approximately 3.5 miles. Drive west on University Avenue. Turn right on NM 292. Turn left at the sign for the plaza.

Cinco de Mayo Celebration (68) and Mexican Independence Day Celebration (69)

Although the Cinco de Mayo and Mexican Independence Day celebrations are held at different times of the year, these lively and colorful events are very similar, so the same photo advice applies to both.

Held during a weekend on or before May 5, Cinco de Mayo commemorates the Mexican army's victory over French forces at the Battle of Puebla in 1862. Mexican Independence Day

San Albino Church, Old Mesilla

is held during a weekend on or before September 16, and it celebrates Mexican independence from Spanish rule in 1810.

Both events are held on the Old Mesilla Plaza and feature traditional Mexican dances, Spanish flamenco dances, food, vendors, and lots of mariachi music. The plaza's gazebo and its surroundings are festooned with bunting and flags and banners, all adding to the events' color and excitement. Usually the first dancing events start around noon and last into the evening. Get there early if you want to photograph San Albino Church before the plaza gets too crowded.

Once the dancing starts, get close to the action and use fill flash to reduce contrast if you are photographing under cloudless skies. Work on taking images of individual *señoritas* and their flowing dresses, musicians in their *charro* (Mexican cowboy) costumes, and wider shots showing groups of dancers. Don't forget overall shots of the crowd and dancers in the foreground, the mariachis and gazebo in the middle ground, and San Albino Church in the background. Watch your corners and backgrounds, however, to avoid unnecessary clutter. Use a fast shutter speed (1/250th second or faster) to freeze the action, but experiment with slower shutter speeds to slightly blur the dancers, thus capturing the movement and excitement of the festivities.

Directions: See directions for Old Mesilla Plaza, above.

Southwest New Mexico Diversions: For a different type of museum experience, visit the New Mexico Farm & Ranch Heritage Museum in Las Cruces. In addition to traditional exhibits displaying artifacts from New Mexico's agricultural heritage, this living history museum features live demonstrations of black-

Mexican dancers, 16 de Septiembre/Mexican Independence Day Celebration, Old Mesilla

smithing, Western roping, saddle making, and Southwestern cooking. And if you visit around lunch time, the Museum Grill offers both hearty fare and spectacular views of the Organ Mountains to the east.

Column, Carlsbad Caverns National Park

VI. Southeast New Mexico

SEASONAL RATINGS: SPRING ★ ★ ★ SUMMER ★ ★ ★ FALL ★ ★ ★ ★ WINTER ★

General Description: Southeast New Mexico's wide expanses are peppered with small but rugged mountain ranges that rise abruptly from the surrounding terrain. Although the region's most famous incident involved reports of "flying saucers" near Roswell in 1947, today the area's biggest attractions are of the natural kind. White Sands National Monument and Carlsbad Caverns National Park offer visitors the opportunity to experience two of nature's unique and spectacular creations.

In addition, Three Rivers Petroglyph Site north of Alamogordo contains what in my opinion is the most impressive collection of prehistoric rock art in the state; and the town of Lincoln, now a state monument, features a large number of well-preserved historic buildings and was once the stomping grounds of Billy the Kid.

> **Noted For:** Carlsbad Caverns, White Sands National Monument, stomping grounds of Billy the Kid, home of Smokey Bear, UFOs
> **Best Times:** Early summer, fall, and during listed events
> **Exertion:** Minimal to moderate
> **Peak Times:** Spring: May; summer: June; fall: September and October; winter: December; during listed events
> **Facilities:** At developed sites
> **Parking:** In lots, on the street, and at trailheads
> **Sleeps and Eats:** Alamogordo, Carlsbad, Roswell, Ruidoso; limited facilities at Capitan, Cloudcroft, and White's City
> **Sites and Events Included:** Carlsbad Caverns National Park, White Sands National Monument, White Sands Balloon Festival, Three Rivers Petroglyph Site, Lincoln State Monument

Carlsbad Caverns National Park (70)

First visited by prehistoric Indians more than a thousand years ago, the caverns near Carlsbad were not discovered by area settlers until the 1800s. Today, two mile-long trails provide self-guided access to Carlsbad Caverns National Park's magnificent rock formations, which include stalactites and stalagmites, soda straws, columns, and many other features that defy description.

The best way to experience the caverns is by first hiking the Natural Entrance Route, a paved 1-mile hike that begins on the surface and steeply descends 750 feet to the aptly named Big Room. (If you would rather not take this hike, an elevator is available that will take you directly to the Big Room). The path is lit with strategically placed footlights, and selected formations are illuminated with flood-lights. Along the Natural Entrance Route you will encounter the Whale's Mouth, Devil's Spring, and a number of other photo-worthy formations. Experiment with different types of white balance and saturation levels (or film types) to determine which combinations produce the best results (the colors will vary because different types of lights—tungsten, fluorescent, mercury vapor—are used to illuminate the caverns). Because you will be shooting in low-light conditions, make sure to use a tripod.

The second self-guided hike, the Big Room Route, is a 1-mile, mostly flat loop that begins and ends at the bottom of the Natural Entrance Route. (It is at this junction that you will also find the elevators, restrooms, and snack shop/picnic area). If you only have time for one hike, do the Big Room. Here you will see rock

Sand dunes and desert shrub, White Sands National Monument, Alamogordo

columns that are 40 feet tall, a depression called Bottomless Pit, the beautifully adorned Totem Pole, and the massive Rock of Ages.

Directions: Carlsbad Caverns National Park is about 27 miles south of Carlsbad. Drive south on US 62/180 about 20 miles to White's City, a junction with a couple of hotels and a campground. Turn right on NM 7 and drive another 7 miles to the park's visitor center.

White Sands National Monument (71)

Located on the southern end of the Tularosa Basin, White Sands National Monument is flanked by the San Andres Mountains to the west and the Sacramento Mountains to the east, and comprises the world's largest gypsum field. Formed by geologic and erosion forces over millions of years, the monument's wave-like, ever-changing dunes are continuously pushed towards the northeast by the area's prevailing winds. The result is a 275-square-mile sandbox of endless vistas, elegant wind-sculpted dune lines, and abstract sand ripples.

For first-time visitors, I recommend driving the 8-mile Dunes Drive to the heart of the dune field to scout photo locations. You will notice there is much more vegetation at the beginning of the drive, less to nonexistent at the end. The cacti, shrubs, and other desert vegetation found at the beginning provide excellent foreground subjects for your compositions, while the heart of the dunes features the tallest dunes and is perfect for semi-abstract and grand landscape imagery. There are also a number of pullouts along Dunes Drive that allow for easy access to excellent photo spots.

If you have a GPS and compass, simply walk out into the dunes and start exploring. Use a wide-angle lens to photograph the grand landscape and consider including distant mountains in the background, but experiment with lenses 100mm and longer to photograph slices of the dunes as they are illuminated by the sun on one side but not the other. Don't forget to look down and take pictures of sand ripples, bug tracks, and even colorful wildflowers (in season). Although the sand dunes photograph well either in the morning or afternoon, mornings are usually best because human footprints are often erased by the wind overnight. If you prefer following a marked trail, try the 4.2-mile Alkali Flat Trail loop near the end of Dunes Drive, which features massive sand dunes and a solitary experience (especially early). For a marked trail with some vegetation, hike the easy 1-mile Backcountry Camping loop, which also offers terrific vistas of the sea-like sand dunes shimmering in the distance.

Directions: From Alamogordo, drive southeast on US 70 for about 15 miles to the park's entrance.

White Sands Balloon Festival (72)

Held every year in September, the White Sands Balloon Festival offers the unique opportunity to photograph colorful hot air balloons as they fly over a sea of white dunes. About 40 balloons participate in the event, taking flight from the middle of the dune field. Because of flight restrictions due to White Sands' proximity to Holloman Air Force Base, the hot air balloons stay close to the launch site, making them easy to photograph.

Arrive at the park early so you can do some scouting before the balloons take flight. Typically the park gates open at 6 AM, while the balloons are launched about an hour later. Keep in mind that the wind will carry the balloons to the northeast, so plan accordingly. While scouting, look for locations that will allow you to photograph the balloons as they take flight right over the dunes. You might have to climb a dune or two before finding a good location. For storytelling images, consider including people in your compositions. A wide-angle lens will allow you to take overall pictures of the mass ascension, perhaps with people in the foreground, while a lens 100mm or longer will let you compose more up-close images of the

Hot air ballon and sand dunes, White Sands Balloon Festival, White Sands National Monument, Alamogordo

Petroglyph, Three Rivers Petroglyph Site

crews, balloons, and other details. Because of the fast-paced action, you will be photographing hand-held, so set your camera to an ISO of 400 or higher.

Directions: See directions for White Sands National Monument, above.

Three Rivers Petroglyph Site (73)

Containing over 21,000 petroglyphs made by the Jornada Mogollon people about a thousand years ago, Three Rivers Petroglyph Site is con-

sidered one of the best rock-art sites in the Southwest. Located on a rocky basaltic ridge rising above the Three Rivers Valley, the petroglyphs depict sunbursts, wildlife, hand prints, masks, and a variety of geometric designs. The site is easily accessible via a short, 1-mile (round trip) trail.

Late afternoon is the ideal time to photograph at Three Rivers, when the sun's last rays rake across the flat Tularosa Valley and softly illuminate west-facing petroglyphs. To the east, the tall and often snow-covered peaks of Sierra Blanca provide a perfect backdrop for wide-angle compositions. A lens 50mm or longer will allow you to take portraits of individual petroglyphs.

Although most of the petroglyphs can be photographed from the site's main trail, if you explore the various unmaintained tracks north of the site, you will find many less-photographed petroglyphs that are as interesting as those along the trail. Regardless of where you hike, be aware that rattlesnakes are common in the area, so stay alert.

Directions: Three Rivers is located about 28 miles south of Carrizozo and some 35 miles north of Alamogordo off US 54. From US 54, turn east on FSR 579 (also known as CR 0B30) near mile marker 97; there is a sign for Three Rivers Petroglyph Site here. Drive 5 miles to the site on the left.

Lincoln State Monument (74)

Once said to contain "the most dangerous street in America" because of residents like Billy the Kid, the town of Lincoln is New Mexico's most widely visited state monument and a National Historic Landmark. Comprised of 17 structures from the late 1800s, most of the monument's buildings are representative of the Territorial-style adobe architecture typical of the day in the American Southwest. Lincoln's historic buildings include the Lincoln

County Courthouse, the Tunstall General Store, and the San Juan Mission Church. Depending on the season, 4 or 6 museums are open to the public. A number of Western-themed events are scheduled throughout the year, including Old Lincoln Days (featuring the "Last Escape of Billy the Kid" pageant) in August. Visit www.nmmonuments.org for more information.

Because of Lincoln's layout, morning or afternoon photography will yield excellent results. I prefer the mornings, when the Lincoln County Courthouse, the San Juan Mission Church, and the Old Lincoln Church are illuminated by the sun. The Torreon (defensive tower) and the Wortley Hotel photograph best in the afternoon. Use a tripod for tack-sharp images of these and other architectural subjects.

After your outdoor photo session (or if conditions outside are not conducive to good photography), duck into the Tunstall Store and work on photographing the general store's interior, including 19th-century merchandise displayed in its original cases. Another option is the Anderson-Freeman Museum, featuring historical exhibits from American Indian prehistory to the Lincoln County War (1878–1881). Photography at all the monument's museums is allowed, but flash is prohibited.

Directions: From Carrizozo, drive southeast on US 380 for approximately 30 miles to Lincoln. From Ruidoso, drive northeast about 24 miles to Hondo. Turn left (northeast) on US 380 and drive 11 miles to Lincoln.

Southeast New Mexico Diversions: For an authentic Old West experience, try a ride on the Lincoln County Overland Stage Company (www.stagecoach.bz). After boarding a replica 18th-century Abbot and Downing Concord stagecoach, participants embark on a scenic ride over the rolling hills north of Lincoln. Forty-minute and 1.5-hour tours are available. Before returning to the 21st century, spend the night at either the Wortley Hotel (www.wortleyhotel.com), formerly owned by Sheriff Pat Garrett, or the Casa de Patron (www.casapatron.com). Both inns are located in historic Lincoln.

Rocking chairs on porch, historic Wortley Hotel, Lincoln

Sandstone Bluffs Overlook, El Malpais

Favorites

Parks

Carlsbad Caverns National Park
Chaco Culture National Historical Park
El Morro National Monument
White Sands National Monument
El Malpais National Monument

Hikes

Bisti Wilderness Area
Ghost Ranch
Bandelier National Monument
Ravens Ridge Overlook Trail
El Morro National Monument

Sunrise Locations

El Morro National Monument
Ghost Ranch
White Sands National Monument
Very Large Array
Bosque del Apache National Wildlife Refuge

Sunset Locations

El Malpais National Monument
Rio Grande Gorge Bridge
City of Rocks State Park
White Sands National Monument
Santa Fe Cathedral

Events

Albuquerque International Balloon Fiesta
End of Trail Wild West Jubilee at Founders
    Ranch
Gallup Inter-Tribal Indian Ceremonial
El Rancho de las Golondrinas Civil War
    Reenactment
Old Mesilla Cinco de Mayo Celebration
Christmas Eve Farolito Walk in Santa Fe

Missions and Churches

San Francisco de Asis, Taos
San Miguel, Santa Fe
San Felipe de Neri, Albuquerque
San Albino, Old Mesilla
Santuario de Chimayó, Chimayó
Santa Fe Cathedral

Nonphotography Places

Georgia O'Keeffe Museum, Santa Fe
Richardson's Trading Company, Gallup
Doc Martin's Restaurant, Taos
Museums on Santa Fe's Museum Hill
International UFO Museum, Roswell
Pinos Altos Melodrama Theatre
66 Diner, Albuquerque

Doors, Pueblo Bonito, Chaco Culture National Historical Park

Radio telescopes, Very Large Array, near Magdalena

Scenic Drives

"The High Road" between Santa Fe and Taos
"The Turquoise Trail" between Tijeras and
 Santa Fe
Inner Loop Scenic Byway between Silver City
 and Gila Cliff Dwellings
Sandia Crest Scenic Byway between San
 Antonito and Sandia Crest
Chama to Cumbres Pass
Alamogordo to Cloudcroft to Sunspot

Personal Favorites

Bisti Wilderness Area
Chaco Culture National Historical Park
El Morro National Monument
Santa Fe Cathedral
San Francisco de Asis Church, Taos
El Rancho de las Golondrinas Civil War
 Reenactment
Rio Grande Gorge Bridge
End of Trail Wild West Jubilee at Founders
 Ranch
Shakespeare Ghost Town
Very Large Array
White Sands National Monument
White Sands Balloon Festival
Cinco de Mayo Celebration in Old Mesilla